B

DATE DUE

AUG 27 '75	APR 4 '86		
SEP 6 '75	APR 16 '86		
SEP 25 '75	SEP 10 '86		
OCT 3 '75	AUG 12 '87		
DEC 10 '75	MAR 0 3 1992		
MAR 16 '76	AUG 2 5 1993		
AUG 30 '78	SEP 0 2 1993		
JUL 17 '82			
FEB 15 '85			
MAR 1 '85			
MAR 15 '85			
MAR 29 '85			

WHERE HAVE YOU GONE,

WHERE HAVE YOU GONE,

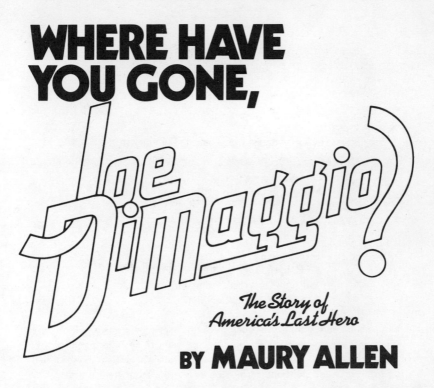

Joe DiMaggio?

The Story of
America's Last Hero

BY MAURY ALLEN

E. P. Dutton & Co., Inc. | New York | 1975

LIBRARY OF CONGRESS CATALOGING IN PUBLICATION DATA

Allen, Maury, 1932-
    Where have you gone, Joe DiMaggio?
    1. Di Maggio, Joseph Paul, 1914-   2. Baseball.
I. Title.
GV865.D5A79   796.357′092′4   75-6523

Published simultaneously in Canada by
Clarke, Irwin & Company Limited, Toronto and Vancouver
ISBN: 0-525-23265-6

FOR MY FATHER
Every man needs a hero. I was born to mine.

Contents

He'll live in Baseball's Hall of Fame.
He got there blow by blow.
Our kids will tell their kids his name,
Joltin' Joe DiMaggio.

— From "Joltin' Joe DiMaggio,"
by Alan Courtney and Ben Homer.
Introduced by Les Brown and his
orchestra in 1941.

Acknowledgments

Most of this book consists of original interviews—with people who knew Joe DiMaggio and with DiMaggio himself. But there were gaps between these accounts, and in order to fill them and present a well-rounded life story, I gratefully drew upon the work of other journalists who have written about DiMaggio.

My particular thanks to Dave Anderson, Arthur Daley, John Drebinger and Lou Effrat of *The New York Times;* to Red Smith and Harold Rosenthal of the *New York Herald-Tribune;* to Joe Trimble of the *New York Daily News;* to Ken Smith of the New York *Daily Mirror;* to Bill Corum and Til Ferdenzi of the *New York Journal American;* to Jimmy Cannon and Milton Gross of *The New York Post;* to Tom Meany of the New York *World Telegram;* to Hal Lebovitz of the Cleveland *Plain Dealer;* to Gay Talese and Roger Kahn for their excellent magazine articles; and to book authors Al Silverman *(Joe DiMaggio: The Golden Year, 1941),* John Underwood *(My Turn at Bat),* Mickey Mantle *(The Education of a Baseball Player* and *The Quality of Courage)* and, of course, Joe DiMaggio *(Lucky To Be A Yankee).*

Thanks, too, to Richard Kaplan, executive editor of the *Ladies' Home Journal,* who moonlights as a sports nut and put me in contact with my agent, Julian Bach; to Julian, for his constant encouragement, faith and understanding; to Thomas B. Congdon, Jr., editor-in-chief of adult trade books at E. P. Dutton, for his enthusiasm, and to Juris Jurjevics, the Joe DiMaggio of senior editors.

A Remembrance

I was fifteen when I first touched Joe DiMaggio. He doesn't remember it. I can never forget it.

It was October 4, 1947, a Saturday, early in the evening. I had spent the afternoon in the Ebbets Field bleachers watching a World Series game between the Yankees and the Brooklyn Dodgers. To get my ticket I had stood in the street outside for thirty-six hours, protecting my spot in line. Rex Barney was pitching a no-hitter for Brooklyn until DiMaggio crashed the ball high into the left-field upper deck, thirty yards from me. The Yankees won 2–1, making me sad, but being there for a DiMaggio home run was thrilling compensation.

Now the game was over, and dusk was settling on Bedford Avenue and Sullivan Place. There were only a dozen kids left waiting—the guards insisted all the players had gone. We hung around throwing and catching a ball in the rotunda, certain DiMaggio was still inside, confident he would sign our programs, our brown paper bags, even— pray God—our autograph albums if we got the pen and the page to him fast enough. Suddenly he was there, walking in rapid strides, two other men with him, his eyes turned toward them, his body huge and magnificent, his black hair glistening. His shoes were so large and shiny.

We closed in, and he signed a few scraps of paper as he walked through. I held my autograph book in my hand but was boxed out by a fat kid with yellow hair. Joe D moved out of the rotunda on to the street, toward a waiting cab. The other kids were yelling, "Joe, Joe, Joe." My tongue was glued to the roof of my mouth. With a desperate lunge I squeezed through and my arm brushed his side and touched his jacket as he bent down into the cab. He was gone.

Maury Allen
Dobbs Ferry, New York
November 1974

WHERE HAVE YOU GONE,

1: Who Is That Guy?

Lefty Gomez has known Joe DiMaggio for a long time —since 1934.

"People didn't see DiMaggio like I did. He just was never a guy who could let down in front of strangers. He was a guy who knew he was the greatest baseball player in America and he was proud of it. He knew what the press and the fans and the kids expected of him, and he was always trying to live up to that image. That's why he couldn't be silly in public like I could, or ever be caught without his shirt buttoned or his shoes shined. He knew he was Joe DiMaggio and he knew what that meant to the country. He felt that obligation to the Yankees and to the public.

"I think about DiMaggio now and it's funny to count the years that have gone by. It all seems like just yesterday, but I guess Joe and I have been connected for about forty-five years, actually, one way or another. I was playing in San Francisco when I was eighteen, and DiMaggio told me later he used to come to those games as a thirteen-year-old kid with the knothole gang to see me play. I was

17

eighteen and he was thirteen. It was a strange feeling later, when we were both with the Yankees, to realize that I was rooming with that kid who used to watch me pitch. Of course, he wasn't thirteen any more, but he wasn't much older either. DiMaggio will always be a kid to me, I don't care how many gray hairs he gets.

"You know it's about forty years ago but I remember the first time I ever saw DiMaggio. I had a big year with the Yankees, won twenty-six games, and now I was back in San Francisco for an exhibition game. They used to play a lot of postseason games out there in those days before the major leagues moved to the Coast. Well, I'm the big-shot local guy pitching in this exhibition game against the Seals. I think we had a team of major-league players from the San Francisco area against the Seals. Lazzeri, Crosetti, and a few other guys were on the team, and now I'm facing this kid DiMaggio for the first time. I don't know who he is and I don't care. I was the star attraction because I had the big year, and the people had come out to see me. Now the first time up this big kid gets a hold of my best fast ball and whacks it like a bullet off the wall in right field for a double.

"The next time up I figure I'd better be a little more careful with him, so I get a pitch a little lower and a little more inside on him, and he hits that one on a line off the wall in right center field for another double.

"Now I'm steaming pretty good. I don't like a kid outfielder from the Seals treating the great Lefty Gomez from the Yankees that way. I look up and our manager, Earle Mack, Connie's son, is coming out to the mound.

" 'Do you know who that kid is?'

" 'No, does he know who I am?'

"Earle tells me his name is DiMaggio, he is the hottest thing in the Coast League, he once hit in sixty-one straight games, and I better work on him like he's a big-league hitter because he will be a big-leaguer very soon. I think I finally got him out the next time, on a ball that he hit near the wall.

"Years later he used to kid me about that game. 'You had a big year with the Yankees; you won twenty-six games. I was just a kid and I got two doubles off you. You couldn't have been so good, Lefty, if a kid like me could get two doubles off you.'

" 'Yeah, Dago, but you couldn't have been too good either. You didn't pull the ball against me.' "

2: San Francisco Days

Small fishing boats were tied up along Fisherman's Wharf almost as far as the eye could see, bobbing with the summer breezes. When Joe DiMaggio was a boy growing up in San Francisco, his father sailed such a boat from the dock every day. The DiMaggios and their nine children depended on its catch.

Tom DiMaggio is the oldest son.

"For years my father had his boat tied up out there. It was called *The Rosalie D,* after my mother, and it went out every morning. He kept that boat sailing for a long time, fishing every day, selling his catch out here on the wharf, patching the boat, making his living from the sea. When it couldn't sail any more he sold that boat and got another."

Tom DiMaggio is a small man, seventy years old, with thinning gray hair and a prominent nose. He has a small brush mustache and looks weathered and tired. When he turns his head to the side, he suddenly resembles his brother Joe.

Tom sat in his small office in the basement of DiMaggio's Restaurant on Fisherman's Wharf, casually attired in a fisherman's green stocking cap, plaid shirt and tan overalls. The restaurant has been part of the family since 1937. He has always run it.

"I don't know why I keep this place going. Joe and Dom have a piece of it, and they want me to sell it. 'What do you need it for?' they ask me. They keep telling me to get out. I can't get out. It's for the tourists. They come out here. They expect it. I struggle. I keep it going. I can't really tell you why."

On some mornings, around eleven o'clock, if he is in town, Joe DiMaggio will come in and sit at the small table on the right, away from the large windows, and sip a cup of tea.

"We had a grandfather, on my mother's side, living around here in a small place called Collinsville. He wrote his daughter—my mother—back in Sicily and told her that things were better. The old man knew that his son-in-law was a good fisherman, that my father could make a living here.

"My father decided to come over here, to stay a year and see how things would work out. When he left, my mother was pregnant with my oldest sister, Nellie. She was the only one of us born over there. My father went to Collinsville first and then he moved over to Martinez across the bay. The fishing was good. He waited a year and then he sent for my mother. She came here and they lived in this small apartment in Martinez. Joe was born there. November 25th, 1914. When he was a baby we moved over here to this side of the bay, to the house on Taylor Street. Let's see, how old was I? Nine, ten, something like that."

For the next two decades the DiMaggio clan lived in a four-room apartment on Taylor Street. Eventually there were eleven DiMaggios in those four rooms.

"Nobody wants to work any more. When I was a kid, we wanted to work. We wanted to get out of poverty. I ran papers, I worked on the boat, I did anything I could to make a few pennies. I worked in a bakery and I got paid two loaves of bread. They were hard, maybe a day or two old. My mother put them in the oven, made them soft, and they were as good as new. Nobody complained in my house."

Tom played some baseball himself as a kid, for semipro teams around town. But he was never serious about the game.

"I was pretty good at it too. I could have played but I didn't like it that much. But Joe—he would run out as a kid and play all day."

"Vince was the first to play and then Joe and then Dom. They all were good at it. We had another brother, Michael; he died as a young man in a drowning accident."

There is a legend that has grown up through the years that DiMaggio's father, knowing little of baseball, fought hard to keep Joe from becoming a baseball player.

"That's a story, like a lot of those stories, just made up through the years. What the old man wanted, what he really wanted, was for Joe to get an education, to make something of himself, to make a living, to get away from the struggle, the poverty we had as kids. That's why he didn't want him to play baseball. He didn't think he could make any money at it. When Joe got to the big leagues and proved he could make money, nobody was prouder and happier than my father.

"You look around, look at the pictures, take your time. I have to get to work now. I'll tell Joe you were looking for him."

In the Pulitzer Prize-winning novel *The Old Man and the Sea,* Ernest Hemingway's main character says, "I would like to take the great DiMaggio fishing. They say his father was a fisherman. Maybe he was as poor as we are and would understand." No doubt the great DiMaggio would have understood. But he might have declined the old man's invitation. "I never liked the smell of the boats or the fish," Joe once confided to his friend, sportswriter Jimmy Cannon. Neither did Joe's pal Frank Venezia, and the two boys, looking for odd jobs so that they could help their families, preferred any other job to fishing. Mostly they hawked newspapers.

Frank Venezia, now a retired teamster, hasn't seen Joe DiMaggio in thirty years, but he still remembers their youth together.

"I was the only friend Joe had. He was really shy then, even more shy than me, and a real loner. If his brothers weren't around, he would sit in the playground and not talk to anybody. He'd talk to me, though. We'd talk about the big league players and about selling our papers.

"We used to sell papers together after school. We'd stop off at the North Beach playground first and play a few innings before going on our routes. Then we'd take off, get on the trolley to the wholesalers, get to our regular corners, and sell our papers. I used to cheat and stop off on the way home and buy some potato salad and eat it. Joe never bought anything. He brought every penny home. Joe's parents were pretty strict. Especially with money. We joined a Christmas club once, fifty cents a week, to save up and have twenty-five dollars at the end of the year. Joe made his deposits every week from his paper money. I skipped a few times. I never lasted out the whole year. I would pull it out in August or September and buy a glove or a ball or something.

"We must have been around ten or so when we saw that Joe was going to be pretty good as a ballplayer. We used to play a game on the street called piggy-on-a-bounce, with a stick and a rubber ball, and Joe would hit it a lot

22

farther than anybody else. He was just naturally good. Of course, his brother Tom was a hell of a ballplayer and was already playing with some pretty good semipro teams, and Vince was playing with some good kid teams. Dom came along later and I was real friendly with him. I even spent one summer with him when he was with Boston.

"Well, anyway, we were playing ball at North Beach, and it got to be time to go downtown for the papers. We used to get together and it would be two for a nickel on the trolley or something like that. Joe knew we had to leave, but I was having too much fun and I didn't want to go. I told Joe to go downtown by himself and I would meet him there. He got pretty mad about that but he went. Then I just kept playing. I never went to the wholesalers and I didn't get any papers that day. Joe had to go there, sell his papers and come back on the trolley by himself. The next day when I saw him he wouldn't talk to me. He was pretty sullen. I just couldn't figure it out. He didn't talk to me for a year.

"After that incident, we passed each other in the street, played in the playground, and sat in school together and never talked. I wasn't mad. That's just Joe for you. He didn't have any other friends. He didn't need any. He had his family.

"We were about fourteen, fifteen, when an olive-oil dealer in the neighborhod named John Rossi told us he would back a team in a sandlot semipro league. We had this team, the Jolly Knights, down at the boy's club, and Joe had played third base and shortstop there. A friend of mine—a guy I called Bat Ninafo because he only wanted to bat and not field—asked me if I could get Joe to play. Joe had always been the first guy picked in all the school-yard games. Everybody knew he could play. I told Bat that Joe was not talking to me. 'Ask him anyway,' he said. So I saw Joe in school one day, and before he had a chance to walk away I told him Mr. Rossi was backing a hardball team and we would have uniforms and new gloves and spikes. He didn't say anything about the fight and he agreed to play."

Playing for the Rossi team, Joe hit two home runs in the playoff game that decided the title and won two baseballs and a pair of gift certificates good for fifteen dollars' worth of merchandise.

"After we got together, we were friends again until he left the city to play professionally. We went to Hancock Grammar together, to Francesco Junior High, and then to Galileo High. Joe got along okay in Hancock and in junior high, but high school was tough. He was really shy, always, but in the lower grades it didn't seem to matter. Every once in a while we would have dances over at the boys' club. You couldn't get Joe to go. I'll tell you the truth, I don't think he knew how to dance."

DiMaggio was so shy around girls that he would rush out of his own home whenever his sisters had female friends over. He was afraid his sisters might introduce him and thereby force him to talk. Rather than take the teasing, he fled.

"Joe had a keen mind. He would have been good at anything he did. He just wasn't interested in school. I think part of it was he was afraid to talk in class. That probably came from his home. His parents were hermits. They didn't come out of the house much; they didn't gossip with the neighbors. My mother, she was out there every day. Joe's parents only spoke Italian. Most of the other families around learned English. I think that had something to do with his shyness. I really can't tell you if Joe spoke Italian to his parents or what they spoke to him. Nobody around there could tell you. Nobody ever got invited inside their house.

"We went to grammar school and junior high school in our own neighborhood with kids like us. High school was different. The school was away from the neighborhood and

24

there weren't many sons of fishermen. There were a lot of kids from the better sections, and they were better dressed than us and had better schooling and seemed to adjust more easily to high school. It was a shock for Joe and me to see these kids in their new jackets and ties when we were wearing the same old clothes we had in junior high.

"We started playing hooky a lot, hanging out down by the docks and going fishing off the pier, and missed a lot of our schoolwork. One day we were in school and Joe hadn't done his work and he wasn't prepared and the teacher threw him out. It really embarrassed him. The teacher was Italian and he began singing a song to me in Italian about how I would be the next to go if things didn't get better.

"When things started going badly in school, Joe became more and more interested in sports. He was already the best kid in the neighborhood in baseball. He could play football good too. We used to play touch-tackle in the streets, and he could throw the hell out of the ball. I had always liked tennis and had played a lot of it. The first day Joe picked up a racket, he almost beat me. He was also very good at cards. We used to play poker for a couple of pennies or the Italian game of seven and a half, and Joe would almost always win. He had this uncanny knack of remembering all the cards.

"After Joe went off to play ball I never saw him again, except for one time in Yankee Stadium, but I followed his career very closely. I never played again after our high school days. I was too small, I didn't really have it, and then I broke my wrist in a fall. That finished me. I'll never forget those days with him. He could hit the ball a mile. He made everything look so easy, it was terrific. He was the greatest there ever was on the ball field. As for his personality, I'd have to say that wasn't too much then."

Things began to get difficult for Joe DiMaggio in his first year at Galileo High School. He felt awkward and uncomfortable with the new kids. He didn't make friends. He was assigned to a class in ROTC when what he wanted was a class in physical education. He reacted by staying away from school for half a year.

"I finally got caught," DiMaggio said years later. "They made me make up the credits and I did. One day I had to go see the principal, and I waited in his office and waited and waited and he never showed. So I left, and that probably made a professional baseball player out of me."

That was 1931, the Depression, a bad time to look for a steady job. DiMaggio, with little education and no skills, worked as a laborer on the docks. He crated oranges. He worked in a cannery. He delivered groceries. He helped load trucks. As he worked, he came to realize that baseball was the one thing he liked to do, the one thing he was good at. He also discovered that people actually could make a living at it.

Tom had played some semipro ball, of course. Also Vince, who had quit school to work in a fruit market and help out the family, had played baseball on Sundays for two dollars a game. Then he had been scouted and signed by the San Francisco Seals of the Pacific Coast League, a fine Triple A team, just a step below the major leagues. He was making a hundred dollars a month.

"I was a cocky kid," DiMaggio recalled. "I figured if Vince could get paid for playing baseball, I could get paid too."

Vince was sent to the Tucson farm club of the Seals and was brought back at the end of the season. Joe played that summer for the Sunset Produce club in a fast semipro league and hit .633 for eighteen games. He did so well with the Sunset team that a professional club, the San Francisco Missions, offered him a contract at one hundred and fifty dollars a month, twenty-five dollars more than was usually paid to untried sandlot kids. They knew a hot prospect when they saw one.

26

DiMaggio went home to talk over the offer with his family. He was seventeen and almost full grown: a lean six-foot two, with long arms to go with his long legs, and a well-muscled body from lifting crates and lugging boxes on the wharf.

His father still thought baseball was nonsense, but one hundred and fifty dollars a month for throwing a ball was more than he himself made working seventy hours a week catching fish. Brother Tom was all for it. He encouraged Joe to sign before they changed their minds.

Joe wanted to talk it over with Vince, who had often told him that if he ever became really serious about the game and devoted all his time to it, he could be an excellent player. Vince had just been recalled to the San Francisco Seals after a .347 season at Tucson. So Joe went down to the Seals ball park to watch his brother play and ask his opinion of the offer. Having no money for a ticket, he peeked through a hole in the fence. A scout named Spike Hennessey, who worked the San Francisco area sandlots looking for talented kids the Seals could sign cheap, spotted Joe at the fence.

"You're Vince's kid brother, ain't you?"

"Yes."

"Never stand on the outside looking in unless it's a jail. Come with me."

Joe was taken to the office of Charley Graham, who ran the team, and was presented with a free pass.

"The kid's a good-looking ballplayer too," Hennessey told Graham.

"Really?" said Graham. "How would you like to work out with the Seals?"

In 1932 the Seals were about as high as a San Francisco youth could ever hope to go in baseball. The major leagues were a faraway dream, an unreal hope for most. And a man could make a good living playing for the Seals. Minor-league baseball was important then, and many ballplayers spent long and prosperous years playing for such teams all over the country. So Joe forgot the contract offer from the San Francisco Missions and went with the Seals.

In the final week of the 1932 season Joe DiMaggio made his professional debut—as a shortstop. He hit a triple his first time up. He did not have a contract and was not paid, but he impressed the Seals enough to be invited to spring training in Fresno, California.

DiMaggio came to that Seals camp in March 1933. He hit line drives all over the place and was signed to his first professional contract at two hundred and twenty-five dollars a month, about twice what the average rookie was being paid. When the Seals opened the season in April he still didn't have a position because he couldn't field at short-stop and he threw horribly. However, he could hit. The manager, Ike Caveney, a wise old pro who had been with Cincinnati, was simply waiting for a spot. An eighteen-year-old kid needed some time on the bench merely to grow accustomed to professional baseball.

About two weeks after the season opened, DiMaggio was sitting on the Seals bench next to his twenty-year-old brother, Vince, who couldn't crack the starting lineup either. Ed Stewart, another rookie, was in right field for the Seals that day. He had hit well in spring training, was a fine defensive outfielder, and was the regular at the position. The Seals fell behind 6–1 and Caveney decided he had his spot. He called Joe's name and sent him up to the plate.

"I went to the plate in a trance," DiMaggio later recalled. "I walked, which was just as well, because I doubt if I could have swung the bat with any force."

The inning ended and DiMaggio jogged back to the bench. He figured he was through for the day.

"Go out to right field, Joe," said the manager.

DiMaggio had played first base, third base, and short-stop as an amateur. He had never played the outfield.

"I've never played the outfield in my life," DiMaggio told his brother Vince.

"I know," said Vince, "but you're going to start now."

Except for one game at first base at the end of his Yankee career, DiMaggio was always to be an outfielder.

The next day he started in right field and got two hits. He was on his way. He began knocking Pacific Coast League pitching around with a vengeance. He batted .340 as a rookie, led the league with 169 runs batted in, had 28 homers, and played in an incredible total of 187 games. Right field was an uncomfortable position for him at first and he made 17 errors, but he showed his marvelous throwing arm early with a league-leading 32 assists.

At eighteen, DiMaggio became an instant celebrity. He was the hottest thing the league had ever seen. It all came to a furious climax when he broke the Pacific Coast League hitting record of forty-nine straight games established by Jack Ness in 1914, the year DiMaggio was born. Joe beat the record by hitting in sixty-one consecutive games.

The mayor of San Francisco, Angelo Rossi, presented DiMaggio with a gold watch after he tied Ness' record. His old teammates on the Jolly Knights gave him a traveling bag, and his San Francisco teammates gave him a check.

"I never really felt any pressure," DiMaggio said of that minor-league streak. "I was just a kid; I didn't know what pressure was, and I was having too much fun."

DiMaggio rested all winter after his impressive year. The newspapers were filled with stories about San Francisco's new star. DiMaggio read them calmly, knowing full well that a .340 in the Pacific Coast League was still a far cry from a major-league job. But now he felt he could do it, in time.

One day a few months into the 1934 season, it looked as if DiMaggio's future in baseball was over. He had played a doubleheader at the Seals ball park, then spent the evening at the home of one of his married sisters. After dinner, he took a cab home. He got out of the cab left foot first—all his weight on it—and went down. His foot had simply fallen asleep.

"There was no twisting," DiMaggio recalled, "just four sharp cracks at the knee and I couldn't straighten out the leg. The pain was terrific, like a whole set of aching teeth in my knee."

The manager of a nearby movie house drove him to the hospital. DiMaggio was told to go home and apply hot towels and Epsom salt packs. The next day he could barely get out of bed. He called his manager, Ike Caveney, and told him he had had a minor accident but would report to the club for the doubleheader scheduled at Los Angeles that day. He was kept out of the lineup but pinch-hit a homer in the second game, limped around the bases, and was ordered back to San Francisco. The team doctor placed the leg in a cast.

Major-league scouts who had followed DiMaggio closely now were doubtful. The kid could hit all right, and he looked as if he would develop well as a fielder—but what about his legs? San Francisco's team made most of its money by selling off its hot prospects to major-league clubs for big prices—forty, fifty, seventy-five thousand dollars. Few clubs would gamble that kind of money on a kid with a bad knee.

The Yankee scouts, Joe Devine and Bill Essick, were the most interested. Babe Ruth, thirty-nine years old, was coming to the end of his career. Having already hit forty home runs in a little more than a season and a half, DiMaggio could be the new power player the Yankees needed to team up with Lou Gehrig.

As stories about DiMaggio's knee problem appeared in the papers, the asking price went down. The Yankees told the Seals they would go as high as twenty-five thousand dollars and five players for DiMaggio, and wanted an extensive examination of the youngster by a doctor of their choice. DiMaggio was dispatched to Los Angeles to be examined by Dr. Richard Spencer, a noted orthopedist. Dr. Spencer concluded that a young, healthy male of nineteen could come back fit from a knee injury of this type and so notified New York. Essick relayed the news to Yankee general manager Ed Barrow, who in turn reported to the Yankees' owner, Colonel Jacob Ruppert, that DiMaggio had had a favorable medical report and could be bought for twenty-five thousand in cash and five journeyman players.*

"Buy him!" barked Ruppert.

In November 1934 the deal was completed. Joe Di-Maggio was sold. He was to play out the 1935 season with the Seals, receive regular medical treatment, and report to the Yankees at St. Petersburg, Florida, in March 1936.

DiMaggio finished his minor-league career in style, with a .398 batting average under Lefty O'Doul, the new manager. He led the league again with 154 RBIs and hit 34 homers. O'Doul taught him to pull the ball—to meet the ball earlier and knock it to left field—an asset that would be a necessity in the vastness of Yankee Stadium.

DiMaggio had no doubts that he would make the Yankees now. "I was cocky, confident, call it what you want," he said years later. "I knew I could play. But I kept it inside myself, inside the shell."

Joe had no reason to doubt himself. He had burned up the tough Pacific Coast League for three straight seasons; he had handled all kinds of pitching; he had learned to play the outfield; and he had batted against many former and current major-leaguers in regular and exhibition games.

* They were third baseman Ed Farrell, pitchers Jim Densmore and Floyd Newkirk, first baseman Les Powers and outfielder Ted Norbert.

It was not surprising that as DiMaggio prepared to leave home for the New York Yankees' training camp in Florida, baseball people already knew all about him.

Frank Crosetti, a thin, energetic little man, was with the Yankees from 1932 through 1948. He retired after forty-four years in baseball, forty of them as a player and coach with the Yankees. Sixty-five years old now, he lives quietly in Stockton, California. In February 1936 he was also making preparations for the trip to the team's spring-training camp.

"I lived over in the Cow Hollow section of San Francisco in those days. Tony Lazzeri lived over in the Italian section in North Beach. He'd sort of watched over me when I came to the Yankees in 1932, being an Italian kid from San Francisco like him, and we'd become real good friends. Tony was a quiet guy, no bullshit, a straight guy and a hell of a player. He had the guts of a burglar and was some clutch hitter, a damn tough guy to get out with two strikes on him in a big spot. I'll tell you, I cried like hell when he died in 1946. He was only forty-two. I lost a great friend.

"Well, anyway, Tony had this beautiful Ford sedan that he'd just bought for the trip to Florida. He comes over the house one day and asks me if I want to drive with him to Florida in it. I'd always taken the train so it sounded like it'd be fun. We both knew DiMag from around town and decided to ask him along. He had a big reputation as a player with the Seals and we'd see him once in a while around San Francisco. DiMag didn't say much, but we knew his brother Vince, and Vince asked me to watch out for the kid. You could see DiMag was really excited being around Lazzeri.

"Tony called DiMag on the phone and set the whole thing up. He told him we would pick him up and to be out on the street in front of his house. DiMag was there on time, all right. As soon as he gets in, Tony tells the kid to come up with fifteen bucks for the trip. We each put up fifteen bucks and I held the money. I think we had to add another five bucks altogether for the whole trip. We had fifty bucks for three guys, eating, sleeping, gas, everything, for maybe ten days.

"I was a quiet guy. Tony didn't talk much, and DiMag didn't say a word. He just sat in the back seat and looked out of the window. His eyes were open wide and he was watching the country roll by. Tony and I shared the driving. We would go two or three hours and then look at the other guy and say, 'Wanna drive?' and we'd shift places. Sometimes that was all the conversation in the car. About the third day I turned to Tony and said we ought to ask the kid to drive. Tony turned to DiMag in the back seat. 'Wanna drive, kid?'

" 'I don't know how.'

"That was it. I don't think DiMag said another thing the rest of the trip."

When DiMaggio arrived at training camp, manager Joe McCarthy welcomed the young man, assured him he had nothing to worry about, and introduced him to the players. With Ruth retired, the leader of the team was the great Lou Gehrig. Gehrig walked over to the youngster and quietly said, "Nice to have you with us, Joe." DiMaggio nodded. It was a big speech for Gehrig and about average for DiMaggio.

Red Ruffing, a big, rough, hard-throwing pitcher, was quick to tease the newcomer. "So you're the great DiMaggio," he said. "I've heard all about you. You hit .400 on the Coast and you'll probably hit .800 here because we don't play night games and we throw in a nice, shiny white ball any time one gets the least bit soiled."

DiMaggio understood the code. A rookie, no matter how

good, was fair game. DiMaggio took it well, spoke only when spoken to, and let his line drives talk for him. And they did. Dan Daniel of the *World Telegram and Sun* took one look at DiMaggio batting and wrote the next day, "Here is the replacement for Babe Ruth."

Crosetti remembered those first days at St. Petersburg.

"DiMag started hitting line drives all over the place. You could tell he had it from the minute he put on that uniform. We had won the pennant in '32 but we didn't win in '33, '34, or '35. We seemed to be missing another power guy to go along with Gehrig now that Ruth was gone. Everybody hoped DiMag could do it.

"There was this one game in spring training when Babe Pinelli was working the plate and DiMag was knocking the ball all over the lot, three or four hits, a couple of home runs. Finally I come up and Pinelli says to me, 'DiMaggio looks like a miracle hitter. Don't he ever make out?' The next time up Joe made out. He hit a ball about four hundred feet and they catch it on him. 'I'm glad about that one,' says Pinelli. 'Now at least I know he's a human.'

"He fit right in with us. He got along good with everybody—a quiet fellow, of course, but a lot of us were. He got along fine with Gehrig; everybody did. Dickey and Ruffing and all the guys liked him right away. He did his job and kept his mouth shut.

"DiMag made the Yankees a new club in those days. You know what? He never got the credit he deserved neither. Joe didn't push himself on the writers. Everybody took him for granted. He just made everything look easy; he had those long strides and he just got to the ball in the outfield or stretched those singles into doubles. I saw him play every game of his life and I never saw him get thrown out going from first to third.

"I look back at baseball now and at playing with DiMag and it seems like yesterday. Forty years. Where the hell did

34

it go? Life is short. I'll tell you one thing I could have done without, that damn night baseball. Screwed up your eating and your sleeping. I miss it, though. I have to admit that. They didn't push me out. I just quit. I decided the night ball and the flying was enough. My wife is mad at me because I'm out of baseball, especially now around spring-training time. But I was fortunate. I enjoyed it. As for DiMag, what a high-class guy."

George Selkirk succeeded Babe Ruth as the Yankee right fielder. He was given Ruth's uniform, number three, and played with the Yankees from 1934 through 1942, then went on to become general manager of the Washington Senators. Today, a handsome gray-haired man of sixty-seven, he lives in Pompano Beach, Florida.

"The thing we heard about most was the boy's knee. There was no great bidding for him because a lot of people didn't think his knee was sound. We were looking for something great because we had heard so much about him. We needed a leader after Ruth left. Gehrig wasn't a leader. He was just a good old plowhorse—went about his way, took his shower, and got dressed and went home. When DiMaggio and Gehrig were in the same room together, they couldn't fill it with conversation.

"I remember that thing with the diathermy machine.* I was in and out of the training room myself a couple of times and DiMaggio was sitting with his foot in that thing. Somebody had changed the gears or fooled with the dials and it was hotter than it was supposed to be. DiMaggio just sat there with his foot burning up. I guess he was too shy to ask why it was getting so hot. I think he finally com-

* A device used in shortwave therapy, the machine generates heat in tissue by the application of high frequency electrical currents via electrodes attached to the patient's body or other means. Commonly used in the sports world.

plained and they got him out of there, and that foot was really burned badly. It was a sickening sight.

"You couldn't help but notice him that spring. He looked like he belonged. He did things instinctively. When he started playing in the season, you could see we started making plays we had never made before. He would never throw to the wrong base. He just did everything he was supposed to do.

"Joe seemed to fit in with the guys right away. He played a little bridge and he was good-natured about being kidded. One of the greatest guys, Lefty Gomez, took care of him. He followed Lefty around like a toy dog. He was the butt of a lot of Lefty's humor.

"He was the big guy we were looking for, the home-run guy, and we started winning pretty regularly after he joined the ball club."

DiMaggio's burned foot continued to bother him as spring training ended. This was to be the first of a long line of serious injuries. The Yankees broke camp and began a two-week barnstorming tour through Texas and the South. DiMaggio was unable to play in any of the games.

The Yankees opened the season in Washington on April 14, 1936. President Franklin Delano Roosevelt, with his son James at his side and several cabinet members and congressmen nearby, threw out the ceremonial first ball and then settled back to watch Bobo Newsom, the Senators' fat right-hander, match pitches with Lefty Gomez. The Yankees had not won since 1932, and Detroit, the pennant winners in 1934 and 1935, were favored again.

The Yankee lineup listed Red Rolfe at third base, Roy Johnson in left field, Selkirk in right, Gehrig at first base, Bill Dickey catching, Ben Chapman in center field, Lazzeri at second base, Crosetti at shortstop, and Gomez pitching.

Newsom and Gomez dominated. Neither team scored

36

for eight innings. Newsom got the Yankees out in the top of the ninth. In the bottom of the ninth, with one out, Cecil Travis lined a single to left field. Then Carl Reynolds hit the next pitch off the left-field wall between Chapman and Johnson to give the Senators a stirring 1–0 victory.

DiMaggio, sitting on the bench, said nothing all afternoon. He just watched his teammates and the game. As Reynolds' drive crashed off the wall and Travis scored from first, DiMaggio turned slowly with his teammates and walked up the ramp into the clubhouse. He dressed and showered without speaking. He went back to his hotel, ate dinner in his room, listened to the radio for a while, and went to sleep easily. His first day in the major leagues had been an unhappy one.

The foot still bothered him when the Yankees returned to New York. Back in the stadium, he tried to run and couldn't. By late April, however, he started feeling better. On the first day of May he took a long batting practice. No pain. Joe McCarthy watched him closely. The next day Joe went through the same routine.

On May 3 he left his hotel room in the Concourse Plaza and walked the short distance to Yankee Stadium. He look the pregame drills, as he had for the last several days. The sky was heavy with rain and the crowd was only eleven thousand. The game was against the St. Louis Browns.

"DiMaggio, you're in there today," said Joe McCarthy.

McCarthy had shuffled the lineup, moving Crosetti from eighth spot to leadoff hitter, dropping Rolfe from the leadoff to the second spot, benching Johnson, and playing the rookie, DiMaggio, in his first major-league game, in left field. Chapman, as usual, was in center field.

A big right-hander named Jack Knott started for the Browns. DiMaggio hit the second pitch he saw in the big leagues for a line single into left. He singled again the second time up, then flied out, grounded out, tripled to left

37

center field, and popped up. He was three-for-six in his first game, had one easy putout in the outfield, and knocked in one run. As the game ended, with the Yankees beating the Browns 14–5, DiMaggio was smiling.

A week later, against George Turbeville (of Turbeville, South Carolina) and the Philadelphia Athletics, DiMaggio hit a four-hundred-foot home run into the right-field bleachers, some fifteen rows up. It was the first of twenty-nine home runs in his rookie season.

3: First Year

Joe McCarthy, the manager of the Yankees, was the dominant figure on the team. A short, stocky man, he had never played a day in the major leagues. He was conservative in his approach to baseball, a disciplinarian who demanded decorum from his players off the field and hustle and intelligence on the field. He had managed the Chicago Cubs to a pennant in 1929, had been replaced by Rogers Hornsby in 1930, and had come to the Yankees in 1931. He won his first pennant in 1932 and was to win seven more. After leaving the Yankees in 1946, he managed the Boston Red Sox. He is a member of Baseball's Hall of Fame. McCarthy is eighty-seven years old and in good health, and lives outside Buffalo in Tonawanda, New York. He seems as crusty as he was more than forty years ago when he first managed the Yankees.

"No, I haven't seen anything as good as DiMaggio since I quit. He was a wonderful player and a wonderful man. I still enjoy watching the game on television. It seems about the same game to me as it was a hundred years ago when

Alexander Cartwright laid out the bases. They still play nine men, though they are fooling with that a little, and they still play three outs, four balls, three strikes. It hasn't changed that much.

"I'll tell you where it has changed. The players have it nicer today—big money, easy living, fancy hotels, fancy airplanes. That's how it's changed.

"I started in this game in Franklin, Pennsylvania, in the old Interstate League out of Niagara University in 1907. They gave me a bus ticket to get down there and that was it. We used to dress in the hotels and take the trolley down to the ball park. Carried all our own stuff too. We were still doing that with the Yankees. I remember when I played a game in Philadelphia once. That was about 1908, 1909, something like that. They had the bats and balls in a suit roll. Players took turns carrying the suit roll. They would walk out of the hotel and call for a Victoria—that was the carriage they had then—and ride to the ball park like that.

"Even when I managed the Yankees and we rode on those trains, we still carried all our own stuff. The players carried their bats with them and gave the porter a quarter to carry their personal bags and put them on the train. I remember Ruth and Gehrig walking off a train carting those suit rolls with their bats inside them. Nobody was too good to share the bats.

"The trains were pretty nice. I always had a good compartment and I could sleep good on the train. I got out just in time. I didn't like the airplanes. I'm glad I didn't have to rush up and down the country in an airplane.

"You didn't want to hear about me. You want to hear about DiMaggio. He was a little timid when he broke in. He never bothered anybody and they didn't bother him either. He just did his work. It didn't take long to figure out that he was going to be something special. He was the best rookie I ever saw break in. There's no question about that.

He looked real good in spring training that first year—what was it, '36—and then he burned his foot in that machine. Well, we knew he could play so we just waited for him to get well. Ben Chapman was my center fielder then and he was a pretty good one. He could really go get a fly ball. DiMaggio had never played center field. I watched him go back on a ball and I knew he could play it. I started him in left field after his foot got better and then I moved him over to right field for a while. I wanted to make sure he was comfortable before I put him in center field. Finally I decided he was ready so I moved him into center field. He never would have become the great outfielder he was if I hadn't moved him. He needed that room to roam in Yankee Stadium. That's the toughest center field in baseball and only the real great ones can play out there. That's a lot of ground for a man to cover.

"Joe proved he could play and we traded Chapman after that. Once he got out there he stayed out there. He did everything so easily. That's why they never appreciated him as much as they should. You never saw him make a great catch. You never saw him fall down or go diving for a ball. He didn't have to. He just knew where the ball was hit and he went and got it. That's what you're supposed to do. The idea is to catch the ball. The idea isn't to make exciting catches.

"Now you want to know about him as a hitter. Well, he was just about the best. He had this open stance and he stood straight up when he hit the ball. Once he got set at the plate that was it. He didn't drop his bat back. Nowadays you see so many of them moving around at the plate and fooling with their stances and dropping the bat just before the pitcher lets go of the ball. How are you going to hit if the bat is moving one way and the ball is coming another?

"I'll tell you what really made DiMaggio a great hitter. He could hit great pitching. Some of them can get two, three hits off the bushers and not much off the good pitchers. Joe got them off everybody. He didn't care who was pitching. Feller, Grove, any of them, he just hit them. He just hit the ball, not the pitcher. And he could do it in the eighth and ninth inning when the game was on the line, and a lot of them can't hit very good then.

"When DiMaggio first started with us I batted him in the third spot. I had Gehrig hitting fourth. Later on I moved DiMaggio to fourth and dropped Gehrig to fifth. Joe didn't worry about left-handed or right-handed pitching in those days. If a man could hit he could hit. DiMaggio and Gehrig could hit; they could hit anybody. They could hit good pitching and they could hit in the eighth inning and ninth inning. After Joe was with us a year or two we started depending on him more. He's the man who made our club go.

"I'll tell you something else about him too. He was the best base runner I ever saw. He could have stolen fifty, sixty bases a year if I had let him. He wasn't the fastest man alive. He just knew how to run bases better than anybody. I didn't want him to steal. I didn't want him pounding into that hard dirt two, three times a game and tearing up his legs, so that's why I never let him steal. Once in a while I would let him go in a tough game if I felt we were facing a very good pitcher and we needed a run badly. I've been in the game a long time. I never saw a man better on stretching a single into a double or going from first to third on a hit. If he went, you knew he would make it. I don't think in all the years DiMaggio played for me he was ever thrown out stretching.

"Wait a minute. I have to take that back. He overran a base one time. I'll tell you about it. It's a funny story. You know Warren Brown, the old Chicago writer? Well, one time he's interviewing me about DiMaggio and we started talking about how good a base runner Joe was, and I told him what I'm telling you now, that he was the best.

"So now the game starts and Joe hits a line drive to left center field. He takes a big turn around first and now he's going for second. You know he will be safe, because if he goes for the extra base he knows he can make it. He gets to second and all of a sudden they make the relay and Joe is too far off the base and he's tagged out. Now, listen, this is the only time I can ever remember him being thrown out for stretching and I decided to ask him what happened. I knew Warren Brown was going to ask me after the game.

"I walked up to him in the dugout. I could see he felt badly about it. 'Joe, what happened out there?' He shook his head and started telling me. 'Skip, I got to second base and I'm watching for the relay and all of a sudden I think I see the ball and figure it's getting away and I can make it to third. When I look again it wasn't the ball. It was a bird that flew by. By that time they got the ball behind me and I'm dead.' Well, I told that story to Brown later on and he sure looked at me funny.

"Joe really studied the game. He thought about baseball all the time. That's what it takes to be great. You can't just think about it when you get to the park. You have to prepare yourself mentally and physically. Joe had this marvelous sense of anticipation. That's because he studied the game. He never made a mental mistake. He never missed a sign; he never threw the ball to the wrong base. His arm was terrific. He didn't throw that many people out because he didn't have to. They just didn't run on him. They just respected that arm so that they were satisfied taking one base at a time when a hit was in front of Joe."

His rookie season, 1936, turned out to be a banner year for DiMaggio. After missing the first sixteen games because of his foot injury, he played in 138 subsequent games, batted .323, hit 29 home runs, drove in 125 runs, scored 132 runs, had 206 hits, established himself as a marvelous center fielder, and led the league in outfield assists. The Yankees won the pennant for the first time since 1932 and beat the Giants four games to two in the World Series. Joe took his five-thousand-dollar World Series share and made a downpayment on a twenty-five-thousand-dollar home for his parents in the Marina district of San Francisco.

That winter DiMaggio signed a new Yankee contract for fourteen thousand dollars, a six-thousand-dollar raise over the previous year. And the fashion designers of America named him to their list of the ten best-dressed men in the country. Since his wardrobe consisted mainly of dark suits and blue ties, it simply meant he was one of the ten best-known men in America.

4: Superman

"We had a lot of fun then," Lefty Gomez remembered, "but we didn't do much laughing when Joe McCarthy was around." Gomez, whose parents named him Vernon but who, among ballplayers, was known as Goofy as well as Lefty, is an extrovert of the first order. One of the least inhibited of human beings, he would hold up a game he was pitching to watch an airplane fly over, or would put rubber snakes in baseball gloves, or administer hotfoots. He loved to talk, tell funny stories, needle teammates and friends, and cut down pompous people and expose sham. A wag, Gomez was also a great Yankee pitcher and young Joe DiMaggio's best friend.

"I think a lot of the Yankee success in those days was due to McCarthy's leadership. He was a tough guy but he really knew the game. We went through a lot of schooling with him. He was always trying to be perfect in everything, on and off the field. He didn't let guys smoke a pipe, and you had to wear a shirt and tie with a jacket on the road. He wouldn't let you get away with things like dungarees and T-shirts, the way some of the players come to the park these days. He couldn't stand shirts unbuttoned and hairy chests showing. He would really get on you for an open shirt. 'You don't go in a bank and see people with shirts unbuttoned and hairy chests,' he would say. He thought playing for the Yankees called for being the same kind of gentlemen who would work in a bank.

"I immediately adopted Joe when he joined us in 1936. He was a kid from the Bay Area and we Bay Area guys stayed together on the Yankees. Lazzeri was the big daddy of us all because he had been around the longest. Then there was Crosetti and me. We called Lazzeri Big Dago and we called Crosetti Little Dago. When DiMaggio joined us we called him just Dago. Later on, the broadcaster Arch McDonald began calling him the Yankee Clipper, and once in a while we called him Cruiser for the way he went after a ball. But mostly it was Dago.

"You gotta remember that this was back in 1936, back before people were so sensitive about nationalities and all. It wasn't meant to be fresh or to run down a guy's nationality. It was just a way of kidding each other, of developing closeness. It was something to tie us together. We didn't mean anything by it. I'm Spanish and Irish and they called me Spic and Mick. It didn't mean anything. We never did it outside the clubhouse where outsiders could hear it. Hell, nowadays they'd probably put you in jail for it.

"All the San Francisco guys were like relatives so we went around together, Joe and Tony and Crow * and me. Then it sort of became Joe and me.

"Joe was sort of a quiet kid then, sort of mysterious; you never knew what he was thinking or where he was. He's a

* Crosetti.

44

little mysterious to this day. He played in the ladies' pro-am golf tournament last year in Las Vegas. I ran into him and told him I'd meet him for a drink after his round was over. I'm waiting and waiting and he doesn't show. Finally I go up to the bartender and ask him if he's seen Joe. 'No,' he says, 'but I've seen Howard Hughes four times.'

"You had to know Joe to really understand his personality. He's quiet but he could be a very funny fellow. I liked to needle him, still do, and he could take it. He would never get mad, just look at me and say, 'Aw, Lefty,' A lot of people who didn't know Joe thought he was conceited. He wouldn't talk much to the other guys or to the writers or the fans. It wasn't that. It was just that he was shy; he wasn't comfortable talking to strangers.

"Everybody who knew Joe in those days knew he didn't talk. I remember a two-week road trip—New York, Chicago, Detroit, Cleveland, and St. Louis. Two weeks, not one word. I'll tell you what he did do. He would take along one of those small radios on the trip and listen to the radio, the big-band music and those old quiz shows, Dr. IQ and things like that. He'd read the sports pages and he'd read— well, he'll probably kill me for this but he loved to read *Superman* comics.

"One day we were walking down the street of some town and he suddenly turns to me and says, 'Lefty, you know what day today is?' I say, 'Yeah, Wednesday.' Then he says, 'No, no, today is the day the new *Superman* comes out.' Every Wednesday there was a new issue. So now he sees this newspaper stand and looks to see if they got comic books. He points to it and wants me to get it for him. He stands off to the side. Hell, he was Joe DiMaggio and if the newsstand guy saw him buy *Superman* comics it would be all over the world. I got one of those faces nobody could ever recognize so he wants me to buy it for him. 'Joe, is this what you want, the *Superman* comics?' He looks around at a couple of people there and he says, 'No, you know I wouldn't buy that.' Then I walk away and he motions again. I finally buy it for him and he stuffs it into his pocket. He spends the night with Superman.

"Mostly, when he did talk, it was about baseball. Nobody studied the game more than Joe; nobody worked harder at it. He also had more confidence than any hitter I have ever seen. He just knew he was good. That was all there was to it. One year he was hitting about .470 into late May or something. Suddenly he looks over to me and asks seriously, 'Hey, roomie, anybody ever hit .500 in this league?'

"I look at him like he's nuts. 'Are you crazy?'

" 'Don't be surprised,' he says.

"There was this one thing about Joe on the field that used to drive me nuts. He loved to play shallow. He wanted to cut off the Texas leaguers. He knew he could go back on the ball. One time he made this terrific catch off Hank Greenberg in Yankee Stadium behind the monuments. He must have run twenty or thirty miles and he catches the ball going away. I'm telling you, Greenberg hit that ball about four hundred and seventy feet or so and got a big out. That was fantastic. Well, the reporters made a real thing of it, of course, and they started writing stories saying Joe was the best center fielder in the history of baseball and he would make them forget Tris Speaker. Everyone regarded Speaker as the best defensive outfielder ever and he always played shallow. The good ones usually do. But Joe was ridiculous. He was always too shallow, I thought, especially when I was pitching.

"Well, anyway, this one time we're playing Detroit. Rudy York is up. He was that big Indian first baseman they had and he could hit the ball a mile if he caught hold of it. I look around and DiMaggio is playing behind second base. He was really in shallow. I got York out on a ground ball or something and when the inning's over I tell Joe I want

46

him to play a little deeper, please. Joe tells me not to worry, he's the new Tris Speaker and he'll catch anything they hit. I tell him I know he can go back on a fly ball, I want to see if he knows how to come in.

"Now it's late in the game and Rudy York is up again. I look around and sure enough DiMaggio is still hugging second base. I put my glove behind my back and I start motioning for him to move back, way back on this big guy. I know he sees my motioning because I turn around and he's still standing out there in shallow centerfield and he's shaking his head no at me. There's nothing I can do so I finally pitch to York. He hits a ball like a shot off the golf tee. It's rising as it passes over my head and it's going about a thousand miles an hour as it goes out to centerfield. DiMaggio has a great jump on the ball as always and is running and running and running. But this time it's over his head and the ball rolls to the fence and we lose the ball game.

"Now I'm really steaming. I know Joe feels real bad about it so I don't say anything to him. Finally he comes over to me and says, 'Lefty, I'm sorry about that ball. I know I should have caught it. But I'm still going to make them forget Speaker.' There's a smile on his face now. 'Joe, I know you should have caught it too, and you keep playing shallow like that, you'll not only make them forget Speaker, you'll make them forget Gomez.'

"Joe was like a kid brother to me when he joined the Yankees. I felt responsible for him the way Lazzeri had felt responsible for me when I came to the Yankees. Good ball clubs are that way. The older players take care of the younger ones. It helps the kids break in. That's the way it was with me. That's the way it was with Joe.

"I think the first thing we ever did together in New York after he joined us was to go to a fight. Joe always loved the fights. Billy Petrolle, the lightweight, was living in the same

47

hotel where Joe and I were staying. Petrolle was one of those religious guys, went to church regularly, really looked like an altar boy. He gives us seats in the front row and we go to the fight and he got his face all smashed up, blood all over him, nose pushed in. He was some sight. We couldn't believe it was the same guy we were seeing every day in the hotel.

"After that I think we went to just about every big fight in New York. Joe got real friendly with Toots Shor, and Toots had a box at the Garden. When I first met Toots he was the head waiter at Lahiff's. I never thought he'd ever wind up with his own place. Toots didn't seem the type. He didn't seem like he cared about running a business. He just seemed to care about being around Joe and the other players.

"After 1939, when Joe married Dorothy Arnold, we used to go out a lot together in New York. His wife was an actress and so was mine—June O'Dea, she was a big musical comedy star when we met—and the four of us got along real well. Joe and I would go to the park together early and the girls would come up later to see the games at Yankee Stadium. In those days I lived on Ninety-first Street on the West Side and Joe was eight blocks away in this big penthouse apartment he had on Eighty-third Street. Joe didn't like to drive so I'd pick him up every morning. He still doesn't like to drive. I don't think he ever learned how to back up. Anyway, each morning I'd get ready to drive to the stadium and we had this signal. I would wave this giant bath towel out of my window and he would see it in his apartment and wave back at me that he was ready. They were always red or green or something like that so we could see them eight blocks away. That meant I'd be at his apartment in ten minutes. I think we went through a lot of bath towels in those years.

"Joe became a big star almost as soon as he joined the Yankees. The man I felt sorry for was Lou Gehrig. He had always played behind Ruth and finally Ruth quit and he had it all to himself in 1935. Now in '36 Joe comes along. Lou had another big year but Joe was the rookie sensation so he got all the attention.

"The relationship between Joe and Lou was very good. They never had a cross word that I know of. They were both quiet fellows and they got along. But it just seemed a shame that Lou never got the attention he deserved. He didn't seem to care but maybe he did. Anyway, I always felt a little sorry for him because of it.

"Joe just seemed to get real popular with the fans in a hurry. I don't know why; it just seemed to happen. All the Italians in America adopted him. Just about every day in New York and on the road there would be an invitation from some Italian-American club for Joe to attend some banquet or some dinner or something. Or the Swiss club wanted him or the Chinese club. Everybody wanted to be Italian if they could get DiMaggio to come to their dinner. Well, after a while he couldn't turn them all down, so he would pick out one here and there and he would go if I would go along with him. We would sit through these boring dinners and finally the guy would get around to introducing all his cousins and uncles and friends in the audience. Joe would get up, the crowd would give him a big hand, and he would say, 'Thank you for inviting me. Now you can hear Lefty tell some funny stories.' Then he would sit down and I would have to entertain them for twenty minutes before we could go home. Then they would load him down with presents and that would be the evening. He'd come home with a dozen shirts or a golf bag or a watch or a toilet set or luggage or something like that.

"One time we were in Chicago and he gets invited to

some dinner in Evanston. I had probably gone to every one of these things with him for five years. This one night I just didn't feel like going.

" 'Joe, you go yourself. I'm going to the movies.'

"He argued with me for a while, but I wouldn't go. I went to the movies and he went to the dinner. I get back to the hotel later and he's back in the room. His stuff is all laid out on my bed—golf clubs, golf bag, shoes, luggage, travel clock, watch, shaving kit, the whole works.

" 'Did you get all that stuff at the dinner?'

" 'Yeah, I did, and they had the exact same thing for you but since you didn't show up they couldn't give it to you.'

"It was the first one of these things I had ever missed and I got shut out.

"I don't know if it was a gag because we have always been good at needling each other. He needles me as much as I needle him. It's been going on that way for more than thirty-five years now. Just a few weeks ago I ran into him accidentally in San Francisco on Post Street. I saw him coming down Post Street, ducked into a doorway, and as he came out I walked up to him and said, 'Good morning, my name is Lefty Gomez. Are you the great Joe DiMaggio?' He just said, 'Go to hell, Lefty Gomez,' and broke up.

"It's funny now with all the golf he plays. He used to get all that golf equipment as gifts in those days and never used it. He would give it all away. He hated the game. He thought any ballplayer playing golf had to be crazy. Now he probably plays every day. I remember when I was with Wilson Sporting Goods and he was a batting instructor for the Yankees in spring training. As soon as he'd see me, he'd hit me for golf balls.

"Joe really relaxes on the golf course, enjoys himself and laughs a lot. He was too serious about baseball to laugh on

50

the field. But he could laugh all day long if something struck him funny off the field.

"This one time I had pitched in Cleveland against Bobby Feller and I went thirteen innings and I got beat 2–1. Well, if you got beat, McCarthy didn't want you to blink your eyes. You just spent the rest of the day being quiet and thinking about it. We got on the train after the game and we were going on to Detroit. I really felt down after that game. I had pitched as good as I could, as long as I could, and we still lost. I was really feeling sorry for myself. Now DiMaggio comes along and he asks me to go up to the dining car for dinner. I told him I didn't feel like going up to the dining car for dinner. I just wanted to sit on the train and look out the window. Joe was trying to get me interested in something and forget about the game. Usually I was always talking to him after he had a bad day and trying to make him forget. This time he was helping me out.

"For some reason or other, McCarthy always put me near his compartment on the train. I guess he wanted to watch me. Well, anyway, DiMaggio is trying to get me to go with him. I'm in no mood to go. All of a sudden he says he wants to show me something. 'Lefty, it's something I've just learned.' He puts his thumb and his first finger on the end of that big nose of his and he begins tweaking it— bong, bong, bong, bong. 'Don't I sound like a banjo?' Well, I started laughing out loud. Hell, he did sound like a banjo. He's going on like that and I'm laughing like hell and all of a sudden McCarthy sticks his head out of his compartment and starts screaming at me, 'I bet you think you pitched a hell of a game today, Gomez.' Well, before he could remind me that I had lost the game I said, 'Well, it wasn't bad.' DiMaggio starts laughing like hell now and McCarthy's face is just getting red. He really didn't know what the hell else he could say to these two lunatics he had

on his team so he just slammed the door of his compartment. I think it rocked the whole train."

Gomez left the Yankees in 1943 to play for the Boston
Braves and then finished up with the Washington Senators.

"I see Joe once in a while now, not as much as I'd like
to. I was always traveling and he was traveling a lot and
we would run into each other here and there, usually at
some golf tournament where he was playing and I was trying to hustle some golf equipment for Wilson. Once in a
while I'd see him in San Francisco and we'd have lunch in
his place or I'd meet him over at his friend Reno Barsocchini's place for dinner. I'd call him once in a while and
his sister Marie would tell me his schedule and I would run
into him here and there.

"I'll tell you, the way I keep up with Joe is through the
papers. Wherever he goes they still write about him. He gets
into these golf tournaments and all these great guys are
there and the guy everybody cares and writes about is Joe.
It's amazing the hold he has on people after all these years.
You would think a whole new generation of baseball fans
had grown up who didn't know him, but they know him just
as well as their fathers did.

"You think about ballplayers and you think about two
or three of them who really will be remembered as long as
the game is played—Ruth, Gehrig maybe, DiMaggio. That's
about the list. There were a lot of great players but only a
few that the public seemed to accept as something special.
I never really could figure it out. Joe never went after it.
Joe never pushed himself on sportswriters; they just felt
they wanted to write about him and the fans wanted to
read about him.

"I guess Joe is different than a lot of the rest of us. We
are known as baseball players and that's about it. Joe always seemed more than just a baseball player. He seemed
like a figure, a hero, that the whole country could root for.

That streak in 1941 showed that. He got up to thirty, thirty-five games and that was all anybody in the country seemed interested in. Joe was the biggest news there was. They moved him from the sports pages to the front pages and I had to tell a lot of strange stories to hide Joe from all the people that wanted to shake his hand or be with him in those days.

"I guess I love the man—hell, I'm not ashamed to say that. I guess I love him like you love flesh and blood. After all, Joe DiMaggio is like flesh and blood to me."

5: Getting Booed

On September 15, 1937, Lemuel F. Parton, a financial columnist for *The New York Times,* explained his dilemma:

> This reporter had in mind a piece for today about Louis Franck, the Belgian financier. On the morning train the talk was too much about Joe DiMaggio, the socking sophomore of the American League. Nobody was talking about war or the stock market—Belgian financiers were the least of their troubles—and the clouts of DiMaggio's bat made a heavier detonation than the guns in China and Spain.
>
> When DiMaggio was signed for the Coast League, his father, a California fisherman, thought the game was football and was afraid the boy would be hurt. Just a rookie last year, he already is being mobbed by children in the streets. I heard a youngster, shouting down another the other day, yell that Joe DiMaggio used a lamp post for a bat. He does use an oversize bat and he is filling out to the specifications of Babe Ruth. Bewhiskered Louis Franck of Belgium seems just small potatoes.
>
> Connie Mack, Philadelphia elder statesman of baseball, rates him as the most skillful of all players in their open-

ing years, not excepting Ty Cobb and Tris Speaker. Whether he is the best player in the history of the game is a question which will be settled in due time. If he tops Ruth's home-run record, and some pretty expert experts figure he may in a year or so, he will be headed a long way in that direction.

The World Series will find his father and mother and four sisters and four brothers hanging over the loudspeaker, listening for the crack of his bat. His mother knows no English, but she knows what a home run is.

DiMaggio won his first home-run title with 46 that second year. He batted .346 and had an incredible total of 167 runs batted in. The Yankees won their second straight pennant and defeated the Giants again in the World Series, four games to one. In the final game of the Series DiMaggio hit a home run in the Polo Grounds off a jug-eared Giant left-hander named Cliff Melton.

DiMaggio was now virtually the most famous baseball player in America. The movies thought they could exploit this fame by signing DiMaggio for a bit part in a film entitled *Manhattan Merry-Go-Round*. A beautiful blond starlet named Dorothy Arnold (*nee* Dorothy Arnoldine Olson) also had a bit part in the movie. DiMaggio had just turned twenty-three. Miss Arnold, from Duluth, Minnesota, was nineteen. They were attracted to each other. A romance began.

DiMaggio had been a popular figure in New York with the fans and the press in his first two seasons. He said little but he played the game so effortlessly, so well, that his deeds spoke loudly. He had made the Yankees a winner again, and in a three-team city like New York—with the Yanks, Giants and Dodgers—competition for fans was vigorous.

DiMaggio's image with the public changed drastically in

1938. After his marvelous 1937 season, he negotiated hard for a huge raise. He wanted forty-five thousand dollars, at that time an outrageous salary for a third-year player.

When DiMaggio presented his demand to Ed Barrow, a short, arrogant, unsmiling man who was the general manager and who negotiated contracts by fear and fiat, Barrow almost passed out with shock.

"Do you know how long Gehrig has been with this club? Well, I'll tell you, thirteen years. And do you know how much he gets? Forty-one thousand dollars.* What have you got to say to that?"

"Mr. Barrow," DiMaggio said, "Gehrig is badly underpaid."

Barrow, a harsh and stubborn man, knew he had a tough cookie in DiMaggio. He also knew he couldn't budge. He told DiMaggio he would be paid twenty-five thousand dollars, take it or leave it. DiMaggio didn't yield. Colonel Jake Ruppert, the beer baron who owned the team, loved DiMaggio's play, but he didn't want to undermine his general manager. He urged DiMaggio to accept Barrow's final offer. No one but Babe Ruth had ever really dared to hold out against the Yankee front office.

All of this was chronicled almost daily in the press. Most sportswriters had a natural allegiance to the club management. Ballplayers came and went, but the clubs continued to subsidize their earnings, entertain them with free meals and lavish parties, and flatter their egos. A baseball writer had status, the kind of status no other reporter on the paper could acquire. The sportswriters would not jeopardize that by siding with a player in a contract dispute. And club owners were close to many publishers. There had been too many examples of sportswriters attacking a club in print

* Bill Dickey, Gehrig's teammate and close friend, remembered the great hitter's best salary as being thirty-three thousand dollars for the last year he played.

55

and finding themselves the next day writing obituaries. So the writers fed the resentment against DiMaggio.

Having no other recourse (the free-agent clause in a baseball player's contract had been ruled inviolate by the United States Supreme Court on three separate occasions), DiMaggio signed in late April 1938. He began working out alone in Yankee Stadium while the team went on the road. He had accepted his twenty-five-thousand-dollar contract grudgingly. The public accepted him grudgingly. When he made his first appearance, DiMaggio was booed. Only twenty-three years old, he had demanded more money than many industrialists were making, and he was looked upon as a figure of greed.

Unlike Babe Ruth, who could pass off his contract battles with a brash comment or an outrageous act, DiMaggio had no other weapons to fight with but his baseball skills. While the public turned on him, he turned inward, concentrating on his game, keeping to himself. A few close friends—Lefty Gomez, Toots Shor, and ticket broker George Solotaire— knew he was stung by the public abuse, but outwardly he remained stoic and aloof.

In his first game not only was he booed but, as if it were punishment, he collided with second baseman Joe Gordon while chasing a pop fly; both men were knocked cold and taken out of the game. After that poor start, he went on to another fine season, with a .324 average, 32 home runs, and 140 runs batted in. The Yankees took the pennant again and beat Chicago four straight in the Series.

Joe was even better the following year, and so were the Yankees. Indeed, the 1939 team may have been the best DiMaggio played with, and even better than the murderous lineup of the Babe Ruth era. A doubleheader against the Philadelphia Athletics on June 28 provided dramatic evidence of just how powerful the team was. In the first game the Yankees had 8 home runs and 27 hits (9 in a single inning, against 3 pitchers) and won with a staggering score of 23–2. The second game was just as devastating. Lefty Gomez pitched a shutout while his colleagues belted five more home runs and got sixteen hits for a final score of 10–0. By the end of the day New York had a record 13 homers, 33 runs, and 43 hits.

The Yankees were hot and, after winning the pennant, they beat the Cincinnati Reds in four straight World Series games to become the first team to ever win four consecutive championships.

DiMaggio was at the top of his career with a .381 batting average (it had actually been over .400 for most of the season until an eye ailment interfered), 30 home runs and 126 runs batted in. Deeply impressed by Joe's sheer brilliance, the sportwriters elected him the most valuable player in the league.

For two years he and Dorothy had quietly dated, and finally Miss Arnold's mother announced their engagement and the wedding date, November 19, 1939.

On that day the entire Italian population of San Francisco seemed to be at Peter and Paul Cathedral in North Beach to witness the marriage of their local hero, the great DiMaggio, and the beautiful blond actress. The crowd had begun gathering shortly before daybreak, and as the hour approached—two o'clock—the street outside the church was mobbed. Police were unable to control the crush. Cars streamed toward the cathedral, causing traffic jams for several miles around. A woman fainted in the crowd, and police had to use their night sticks to clear a path to the ambulance.

The wedding was delayed more than half an hour because the bridesmaids couldn't get near the cathedral. Fifteen minutes after the scheduled start Dorothy Arnold arrived, breathless, with her father. Joe's brother Vince couldn't reach the front entrance of the church. He pushed his way to a side door, held the door open for his wife, and was almost trampled by gate crashers barging past. One man entering through the front door with an invitation jostled half a dozen other people in with him, telling the harried guard that they were all his family. Another man showed up with an invitation that was forged; he later admitted he had paid a hundred dollars for it.

After much confusion, excitement, and noise, the ceremony began. Miss Arnold, who had completed instructions as a Catholic three days earlier, was a radiant bride. She had just turned twenty-one. DiMaggio was six days away from his twenty-fifth birthday.

6: The Crowd at Toots'

Toots was not his given name. He was born Bernard Shor but his father called him "my little Toots." The nickname stuck. As Toots Shor he ran a restaurant on Fifty-first Street in Manhattan. By the late 1930s it was America's most famous hangout for sports stars, show business personalities, and political figures. A large, brash, garrulous, always warm and comical man, Toots Shor became more famous than many of the famous people who came into his place.

"It was the first joint run without music. In those days that was unheard of. When the customers ate and drank they expected to be entertained."

Shor taught them to entertain themselves by looking at each other, by spotting famous athletes, movie stars, and politicians, and by drinking, arguing, and sometimes fighting with the host. Shor was loud but he was lovable. The famous came in because they liked the fuss he made over them and the way he forced the other guests to pay homage. The ordinary people came in because on any given night they could see Joan Blondell, Jack Dempsey, Bill Corum, Mark Hellinger, or Joe DiMaggio.

"Yeah, I guess I'm really out of the business now. I miss it, sure, but what the hell, I'm too old for that racket now anyway. The place was good to me. You know, I had a drink with seven Presidents.

"Mr. Hoover used to come in a lot after he was President. A quiet guy, never said much. President Roosevelt stopped by a couple of times after he became President. President Truman came in a lot when he was a senator and Vice-President. He could handle a belt. I think he drank bourbon. He always had some friends with him. Never bothered anybody. I don't think anybody ever knew who the hell he was in those days, you know, just a little guy with glasses.

"President Eisenhower was in the joint often when he was at Columbia. He would be joined by his friends from the Army—General Arnold and General Bradley, guys like that.

"President Jack, that's what I always called him, used to come in a lot when he was a senator. What a handsome devil. Always sunburned. Bobby once in a while too, and Teddy. And the old man was here years ago.

"Johnson came in a couple of times, but the guy who came in the most was President Nixon. He is really a sports fan. He worked in New York, after he was the Vice-President, and he would come over from his office and have lunch and have a drink and talk sports with the guys, whoever was around—Frank Gifford, Alex Webster, Kyle Rote, Charlie Conerly. All the Giants used to come in regularly.

"Yeah, I guess they all came in here. Presidents and kings and athletes and actors and all of them. Chief judges too. Earl Warren was one of my best friends.

"Let's see, where was I? Oh, Yeah. You wanna know about DiMaggio, that crumb bum. He came to New York in '36 and that's when I met him. Babe Ruth and Jack Dempsey used to hang around the joint a lot. Dempsey was the greatest American hero of all time. You're too young to remember the 1920s, but nobody was bigger than Dempsey, nobody, not Lindbergh, not the President, nobody was bigger than Dempsey. I'll tell you who could have been bigger than Dempsey, only one man. Joe DiMaggio could have been bigger than Dempsey. If Joe DiMaggio had stayed in New York every winter instead of going back to San Francisco, Joe DiMaggio would have been bigger. He would have been the greatest hero America ever produced. As it is, he probably is the second greatest, only behind Dempsey. Dempsey is a great man.

"Anyway, Joe was living over at the Mayflower Hotel then, on Sixty-first Street and Central Park, and a guy by the name of Gould lived there in the same building. Gould was a fight manager and in 1936 he was managing Jimmy Braddock, the heavyweight champion of the world. One day Gould introduced Joe to Braddock. Braddock was coming over to my joint—I was at Lahiff's then—to have lunch with Dempsey. He brought the kid, DiMaggio, along. That's how I met him. We hit it right off. Joe was just a great guy, very humble, very shy, but he was very wonderful to my family. My wife always loved him and the kids are crazy about him.

"He started coming by all the time after that. We got real close. He stayed at my house in New Jersey over at Monmouth a lot during the summer, and I'd drive him over to the ball park every day and then go over to the joint. He'd play the game—they only played day games then—and he would come over to the joint for dinner and a couple of belts and then we'd go back to Jersey.

"If the Yankees had won, he would come into the place

and sit at his regular table and I'd eat with him. Nobody bothered him. Everybody would look at him, but nobody would bother him. In our joint if a guy wants to give autographs, fine, but if he doesn't, we don't let the customers bother him. All the waiters knew how to handle that. If the Yankees won and he had a good day and was feeling all right physically—Joe was hurt a lot because he played so hard—some of the sportswriters would come over. He never pushed himself on them; they would just come over. See, that's what changed in New York. They had day ball, and they would all come in after they had written their stories and have a few belts before going home, and sometimes maybe they didn't go home. Joe would sit there, he wouldn't say much, just listen to those lies. He loved Looie Effrat from the *Times.* Looie made him laugh a lot, and Jimmy Cannon was probably his closest friend—they would spend a lot of time together. He admired Bill Corum and Granny Rice and Arthur Daley and Red Smith. He used to love to sit and listen to Red talk. He never had to be afraid of those guys: they would never write anything he told them in the joint. He knew they were off duty and he was off duty.

"I remember one time little Frankie Graham from the *Journal* was in the joint. He had an appointment to interview Alex Webster. He was the running star of the Giants then, and DiMaggio happened to be in the place. Graham came in and Alex was sitting at a table over on the side and he kept looking at DiMaggio. Finally Graham asked Webster who he was looking at. Webster said he was looking at DiMaggio and he had always been his hero, and he asked Frankie if he knew him. So Frankie took him over to meet Joe. His eyes were popping out of his head. Alex was the biggest football player in New York then, but when he was introduced to Joe he was like a little kid. Joe was his hero. That was one of the things about Joe. He was everybody's hero. Still is. When he walks into a restaurant or a room now, everything stops. Joe DiMaggio is the biggest there is, except maybe for Dempsey, like I said.

"Joe was a different guy on those days when the Yankees lost and he had a bad day. He always thought it was his fault. Keller could go oh-for-four or Henrich oh-for-four or Raschi or Reynolds could get bombed, it didn't matter. If the Yankees lost, Joe thought it was his fault. He'd come by on those days and would send the doorman in to get me. Wouldn't even come in the door. He would stand outside and sort of hide, hoping nobody would see him. Then the doorman would come up to me and say, 'Joe's out there.' I always knew what he wanted. I would go out and we would just walk. Up and down the street, up to Fifth Avenue to look in the windows, just walk. No talking, not a word said about the game or my family or anything. He just felt like going for a walk. Then we would go back, he would say good-by, and that would be it until the next day.

"He could really be moody when he was going bad and the team was losing, or if the team was losing and he was hurt and couldn't play. One time Boston was in town for a series with the Yankees, and Joe and I had made a date with his brother Dominic to have dinner at my joint and then go out to a few places around town. It was a big deal for Dom. He was just a kid then. That was the day Dom robbed him of two triples with two terrific catches way back in center field in Yankee Stadium. I knew what to expect. All of a sudden here comes a phone call from Joe. 'I'm not going out tonight.' I tried to talk him out of it. Joe was stubborn that way. That was it. I just called Dom and told him not to bother to come down to the place. I told him I couldn't go out. I didn't want him to know it was Joe. He probably did. He knew his brother.

"Joe knew he was moody. He could sit around sometimes and he would watch Lefty Gomez, his best friend, and

62

Lefty would be drinking at the bar and telling stories to the sportswriters and everybody would be having a hell of a time. 'Toots,' Joe'd say, 'I wish I could be like Lefty, but I can't.' Nobody could be like Lefty.

"Joe's loose now, and he can stand up and make a speech or gab with the sportswriters. He couldn't do it then. Every once in a while he would loosen up. He always got along good with Jackie Gleason. Gleason could make him laugh just standing there. We used to spend a lot of time together—Gleason, Joe and me—in Florida. Every once in a while we would make the rounds of some of the joints. Gleason puts on that he can drink more than any man in the world. Don't let him fool you. He's an amateur. One night Gleason, Joe, and me start out at El Morocco. In those days that was a plush joint. We had a few there and a few some place else and a few some other place. On any given night Joe could go head to head with anybody. He was mostly a beer drinker, but every once in a while he'd start with the Scotch and he could hold his own. This one time we went about all night and Gleason was gone and I was gone and Joe was still there. The only difference was, we didn't have to go play center field the next day. Joe did. I was at the game. Joe Cronin was still playing then and he's one of my great pals. He comes over to the stands and he says, 'I just saw your friend Joe and his head is down. You guys must have worked him over pretty good last night.' I was starting to feel bad. Then the game started and Joe got a triple the first time up for two runs and the Yankees beat the Red Sox about 14–4 or something like that, so I stopped feeling bad.

"The thing about Joe in those days was he never realized how big he was. I think he knows how big he is now. I think he's very conscious of his image, of what a hero he is, and he guards his image carefully. In those days it was all a surprise. We'd go out and they'd make a fuss and Joe wouldn't even see it. One winter, I think it was the winter after Dorothy had little Joe, they stayed in New York for about a month or so. We'd go out every night to dinner, Joe and Dorothy, Baby, and me, and all these café society people would see him and start whispering, 'There's Joe Di-Maggio. There's Joe D.' It was as if he didn't hear it. If he did, it didn't make any difference.

"Did I tell you how I cost him about twenty thousand dollars? That was the winter of '48, and Joe was making about eighty thousand with a bonus deal he had. He was getting ready for a new contract for '49. The Yankees had offered him about eighty-five thousand with a bonus. I told him to ask for a flat one hundred thousand dollars. He was the only guy since the Babe that was bringing them into the ball park, and he was entitled to it."

The Yankees finished third in 1948 but DiMaggio had been brilliant. He had batted .320 and led the league in home runs with 39 and runs batted in with 155. He had earned a huge salary boost and asked for it.

"It wasn't just the money," said Toots, "it was pride. That one hundred thousand meant a lot. Nobody else was making it. It would make him the highest-paid player in history. I didn't think it was right to take a chance on an attendance thing. What if the Yankees had a bad year?

"It was Saturday and Joe was sitting in the place. In come Del Webb and Dan Topping, the Yankee owners, and George Weiss, the general manager, for lunch. I know it is the middle of these tough negotiations, so I tell Joe to sit with them. I don't want him slighting his boss. 'No, I'm sitting with you,' he says. Joe had more guts than anybody. He didn't care about show. He was with me and that was it. Now, everybody sort of gathers at the bar later, and they all get their load on. Joe starts asking Topping about salary. Topping tells him to come up to his apartment on Sunday night and they would talk about it. Joe goes over to Topping's apartment at 405 Park Avenue and they talk some more. Topping was married to Sonja Henie then and I think he wanted to impress her so he says okay for the hundred to Joe. He just has to get Webb, his partner, to go along. Right at that moment Webb is in my place and I'm working on him. He doesn't want to give Joe a penny over ninety without a bonus deal. 'Del, isn't it worth another ten G's to you to get your picture in the paper with baseball's first one-hundred-thousand-dollar player?' I think that got him. Later on Joe came back with Topping and we all got another pretty good load on, and we decided to announce the hundred-thousand-dollar contract the next morning at my place. It was a hell of a show. Then the Yankees went on to draw another 2,200,000 fans, and Joe would have made one hundred and twenty. He kidded me for a long time about blowing some money for him.

"If Joe was playing now he would be making four, five, six hundred thou; he's so much better than any of them. Aaron's a great player but he doesn't bring them in. Babe brought them in, Joe brought them in, and Mickey brought them in. Nobody else. Those guys should be paid whatever they want.

"I'll tell you what made Joe great. I asked him one time. He said anticipation. That's what did it—figuring out the play before it happens. Joe could do that. That's why he was in front of so many balls when the others were diving for them. That's why he was such a good curve-ball hitter. He knew when the picther was going to throw a curve ball.

"Even when he was at the end he was still anticipating. He still knew the game better than any of them. That's why he could play hurt. In 1949 Casey Stengel was the manager. Joe had that heel operation after the '48 season and he hadn't played a game for Stengel yet. Now the season starts and the Yankees are in first place. They are going up to Boston and the Red Sox are driving at them. They

65

got Ted Williams and Doerr and Pesky and all those guys. If they get ahead we'll never catch them. It's late June now and Joe is thinking about playing. He goes down to Baltimore and sees some big doctor at Johns Hopkins. The doctor fixes him up with a shoe. Joe says, 'I think I'll play up there, Toots.'

" 'Why not? You look better striking out than any of those crumb bums hitting the ball.'

"He plays and hits four home runs in three games and the Yankees sweep the Red Sox. I'm sitting in the Polo Grounds each day watching the Giants. I got this usher running up to me each inning with the Yankee score. I was really happy after he hit the last one. I knew he'd be good the rest of the way.

"I think the greatest day Joe ever had was in Yankee Stadium against the Red Sox. The Red Sox had to win one game to win the pennant in '49. Joe had been sick with pneumonia. He didn't know if he was going to play or not. I told him, 'Joe, start or you'll never forgive yourself, even if you can't walk.' He started and got a big hit and the Yankees won the game and won the next day, and that won the pennant. I remember calling Red Patterson, the p.r. guy, just before DiMaggio was about to be introduced. 'Don't let anybody shake hands with him. He's too sick. That will take all the strength away from him.' He played great even though he was weak. The last day the Yankees are leading in the ninth and Bobby Doerr hits a ball past him in center field. Normally Joe puts that in his pocket but he is so weak from the sickness he can hardly move. The ball goes by him and Joe stops the game and takes himself out. That's the kind of class he had. He did what was best for the team. He wasn't worried about Joe DiMaggio. He was worried about the New York Yankees. How many of them think that way today?

"We don't have any ballplayers like Joe today. It isn't just the greatness. It's the way he played, the style, the dedication to the game. Now they think of the big salaries, and they don't want to get hurt, and they just wait out that pension time.

"There never was a guy like DiMaggio in baseball. The way people admired him, the way they admire him now. Everybody wanted to meet Joe, to touch him, to be around him—the big guys too. I'm not just talking about fans coming into the joint. Joe was a hero, a real legitimate hero. I don't know what it takes to be a real hero like Joe. You can't manufacture a hero like that. It just has to be there, the way he plays, the way he works, the way he is, the way people related to him. Take Gleason. Nobody was bigger on television than Gleason. But Joe was a hero to him. Jackie kidded the pants off him; he used to call him Fungo, but Joe was a real hero to Jackie. Still is. That's the trouble with the country today. We don't have any real heroes any more, just got ballplayers and guys in show business and guys in politics but we don't have heroes, not like the kind of heroes Dempsey and DiMaggio were in their day and the way they still are. They can halt business on Fifth Avenue by walking down the street. How many guys can do that?

"Joe was a hero to his own teammates—Keller, Henrich, Page, Lindell, all of them. Lindell—hell, the Yankees won the pennant in '49 when he hit a home run in the last game. Do you know where he was living then? He was living in DiMaggio's apartment. Joe had taken care of him. Lindell was my kind of guy. He had some bum in him. He liked a good time. He was letting it get a little out of hand and Joe saw that the Yankees were going to lose a hell of a ballplayer. Lindell could have been great with a little more discipline. Anyway, Joe got him in line that year, took him under his wing, and Lindell hit that big home run to win the pennant. Joe did things like that to help the Yankees win.

People never knew that; people never knew what a team man he was, how he would take a hundred-dollar bill out of his pocket and give it to a guy if he needed it badly. Nobody ever knew. They all admired him. They all wanted to be like him.

"You know that famous story about how the Yankees got Allie Reynolds? Larry MacPhail was running the club in 1946. DiMaggio was at the Series, Boston versus St. Louis, and he was sitting with me and MacPhail. MacPhail was trying to make a deal with Cleveland. They had offered the Yankees any pitcher except Feller for Joe Gordon. They wanted Gordon to play with Boudreau. Everybody thought they would really be something together. MacPhail asked Joe what pitcher to take. Everybody figured Joe would say Red Embree, the big right-hander. DiMaggio told MacPhail to get Reynolds. Reynolds was a losing pitcher with Cleveland the year before. Joe saw something nobody else saw. They bought Allie Reynolds and he was the best pitcher they had for the next ten years. Gordon went over to Cleveland. He tried to become the Joe Di-Maggio of Cleveland. One night they were playing us and Gordon is in the joint and it's after twelve and he is supposed to be in bed. I told him, 'You better go home. You think you're the Joe DiMaggio of Cleveland? You can stay out past twelve? You can't. You can't break in this late in life.' They all wanted to be like Joe in every way.

"I'll tell you something else. Joe's responsible for me giving up betting. Remember, I lost my first place gambling and betting and all that. Well, I think it was 1942 and Commissioner Kenesaw Mountain Landis came into the place. We start talking and he asks me if it's true that I'm betting on baseball and football and all sports. I had to say that it was. He said that my place was associated too closely with sports and if I wanted those players to keep coming in there, I had to quit gambling. I didn't care so much about those other guys but I wouldn't do anything to embarrass Joe. I told Commissioner Landis that I wouldn't make another bet, no, sir, and I haven't. I didn't want people to come into my place and see Gifford or Webster or Conerly and then see them miss a pass or a punt and say, of course, Shor knew that was going to happen and he laid it down on the other guys. I wouldn't embarrass my guys like that. So I gave it up. I lost my first place because I was gambling, but I sold my second place. It was one of those deals where you sign a piece of paper and you are an instant millionaire.

"Joe was the kind of guy that made everybody around him better. The players were better for having played with him and everybody was better for just knowing him. One year Charlie Keller, who Joe really loved, was having a tough time. Charlie was hurting or something, but anyway he was down around .200 and Joe was getting sick over it. All of a sudden Joe's average started dropping. He went from about .350 to .310 in two weeks or something that. He is in the place one night and all he's talking about is Charlie. 'Charlie isn't hitting. Charlie isn't feeling good. Charlie isn't holding his hands right. I gotta figure it out. I gotta help him.'

"I just looked at him. 'Joe you've gone down some forty points since Charlie's been in the slump. I bet if you forget about Charlie and start hitting yourself you'll both hit.'

"Sure enough, Joe said he would let Charlie work his way out of it himself. There were other good players on the club and the Yankees could carry one guy in a slump but they couldn't carry two. All of a sudden, Joe starts hitting like crazy and, slowly but surely, Charlie starts hitting, and that's that. The Yankees took off and won by seventeen games or something.

"Joe was like that. He was more concerned about his teammates and other people than he was about himself. If Joe had a great day and the team lost, he'd never smile. If

Joe had a terrible day and the team won, then you would think Joe had five-for-five. He was just a great team player as well as being just a great baseball player himself. I miss seeing him in the game, chasing a ball or hitting it or running those bases. That was some thrill.

"I guess I've told you everything I can remember about Joe. He's the best ballplayer I ever saw, the best anybody ever saw. He's a nice boy. He's the same guy today I knew thirty-five years ago, very decent, very strong, good morals, good family instincts—his family is everything to him. He's a real hero—mine and everybody else's."

7: Playing Against DiMaggio

Like DiMaggio, Hank Greenberg, the great slugger of the Detroit Tigers, was a right-handed hitter. He hit fifty-eight home runs in 1938, a record for a right-hander. He led the league in runs batted in in 1937 and 1940 and was the home-run leader in 1938, 1940, and 1946.

Signed with the Tigers in 1930 as a big first baseman, Greenberg led them to pennants in 1934, 1935, 1940, and 1945. When sportswriters considered the annual races for home-run leadership from 1936 through 1940, they inevitably narrowed it down to Greenberg and DiMaggio.

"When I think of DiMaggio I think of the rivalry between us. I always read the box scores of Yankee games the first thing each day. I wanted to see what DiMaggio was doing. The other guys on the Tigers would kid me a lot about it. 'Hey, Hank, Joe knocked in seven runs yesterday; you'll have to get eight today to stay ahead.' I don't know if he was concerned with my records. I never asked him. But I watched him in the paper every day. I knew that if I wanted to lead the league in home runs and runs batted in, I had to beat DiMaggio. If we wanted to win, we had to beat the Yankees.

"The only times from 1934 on through 1940 that the Yankees didn't win the pennant we won the pennant. That was it, just our two teams. That was some rivalry. We knew what every game with the Yankees meant to us. We worried about them. I'm sure they never worried about us. The Yankees never worried about anybody. If we won they figured it was an accident.

"Baseball was different when I broke in. The rivalries were tougher and more sincere. The pension business has changed all that. Now they are all friendly, all working together to increase their pensions. They trade players more now and it doesn't seem as important to win. The high salaries took away a lot of the desire. When I played you wanted to win so you could make that extra twenty-five hundred or three thousand dollars in Series money.

"Players didn't talk a lot to opposing players in those days. I remember when I broke in, in 1933. I played that whole season and about half of the 1934 season. I got a base hit against the Yankees at the stadium and stood at first base. Lou Gehrig had seen me a hundred different times by then. He suddenly looks at me and says, 'Aren't you going to say hello, kid?' I almost swallowed my Adam's apple and I said hello. That was it, just a quiet hello, no big conversation. I didn't know what else to say.

"Opposing players would come up through our dugout in Detroit. That's where both clubhouse were. They just dressed, walked through your dugout, and got on the field. Nobody ever talked to them. The only opposing player who ever really talked a lot was Babe Ruth. He would come into our dugout, sit down, light a cigarette, and start telling our guys stories. He was like a big Santa Claus. Everybody would sit over in the corner of the dugout and he would go on and on about some party he had been to or some show he had seen or some girl he knew. He would just go on and on while the other Yankees were on the field working out. When he felt like he wanted to take a few swings, he would just get up and walk into the cage and hit. I don't think there was ever a ballplayer that didn't love him.

"When Joe came up in 1936 he used to walk through our dugout and go right on to the field. He never turned his head; he never said hello. He just went about his business. It really wasn't unusual. Most players were like that in those days.

"The rivalry between Joe and me—now I'm not saying Joe felt the same way—really was something from '37 to '40. That's about when I was at my peak, before the war, and I was trying to win the home-run title and the RBI title every year. I didn't run well enough to get into the race for the batting title.

"I always believed that RBIs were the most important statistic in baseball. I batted behind Charlie Gehringer and I would say, 'Charlie, you get them to third and I'll get them in.' And that's about the way it worked. Gehringer was a tremendous ballplayer. He was magic in the field and he never had a bad day at bat. Me, I used to have days when I would strike out two or three times or pop up or just not hit the ball good. Charlie almost never struck out. He hit the ball hard three times out of four. It seemed like he was getting two hits every game. If he didn't get a hit, he was hitting a ground ball behind the runner and moving a guy to third, where I could knock him in.

"The players on the Tigers kidded me a lot about the rivalry with Joe. They'd catch me reading the Yankee box scores a lot and they would always needle me when the Yankees had a big inning. One time we were playing in Cleveland and the Yankees were at home against Boston. We look up on the scoreboard and the Yankees had four runs in the first inning. Everybody started telling me that DiMaggio must have hit a grand-slam home run in the first inning. I had a big day, a couple of doubles, maybe four runs batted in, and two or three hits, and we won big. The first thing I do when we get back to the hotel is buy the paper. There it is in a headline: 'DIMAGGIO GRAND SLAM GIVES YANKEES WIN.' Well, that took a lot of joy out of the big day for me. I knew the next day I'd have to go out there and have another big day. If I wanted to top DiMaggio I couldn't ever have a letdown. DiMaggio was like Gehringer. He never seemed to have a bad day.

"The rivalry was really talked about a lot in New York. When we came into town there would always be stories comparing our seasons—who had the most home runs, the most RBIs, and so forth. I was a kid from New York and a Jewish player in a city with the big Jewish population, so I got a lot more attention probably than I deserved. Gehringer was a great player and they hardly ever wrote about him in New York. That's probably why people never did realize how good he was. I think DiMaggio was the best all-around player I ever saw, but Gehringer wasn't far behind.*

"In my time Ruth was the most awesome figure at the plate I ever saw. We always tried to pitch around Ruth. You couldn't pitch around DiMaggio because there wasn't a weak spot in the lineup. They could all kill you: Gehrig, Dickey, Henrich, Keller, Gordon, all of them. Joe never was fooled by a pitch either. I was fooled a lot because I had such a hard swing. Once I committed myself that was it. DiMaggio was a great curve-ball hitter. He had that knack of waiting on the ball and, if it was a breaking pitch, hitting it at the last instant after it broke.

* Gehringer, a Hall of Famer, was considered the best-fielding second baseman ever and had a lifetime average of .320, with thirteen seasons over .300, in the thirteen years between 1927 and 1940.

"Maybe Ted Williams was a better hitter than DiMaggio, but I'm not sure. I have to give the edge to DiMaggio on one account. He never ducked the issue. He was up there to hit. I used to fault Williams because he was the big guy and was supposed to drive in the runs, and if a pitch wasn't perfect he would take a walk and let Vern Stephens drive the run in.

"I used to get mad at Gehringer for that too. He also had to have a perfect pitch to hit. He would stand up at the plate, go three-two on the pitcher, and start fouling off half a dozen pitches that were close to the plate. He was a left-handed hitter and I was a right-hander and I would have to face those tough right-handed pitchers—Johnny Allen, Red Ruffing, Monty Pearson, guys like that.

"DiMaggio, he would hit that ball on the corner, take that short stride, and hit a ball off the plate. He would get a double and knock in two runs instead of taking the walk to load the bases and putting it up to the next guy.

"There was something else about DiMaggio that made him great. The pitchers couldn't intimidate him. They threw at his head a lot, especially when he first broke in. He would just move his head back out of the way of the pitch and never move his body. He'd never say anything. He'd never make a face; he'd never let the pitcher know it bothered him one single bit. He was absolutely fearless. The great hitters are that way. Then there are the other guys like Willie Mays. You throw close to him, his body goes one way, his hat goes another, his bat goes a third. There's a lot of dust flying and it's a great show. But I don't think it helps him hit. One thing about Joe. He was always concerned with how he appeared to the fans and the other players on the field. Everything had to be right with him, from the way his uniform fit to the way he hit the ball. Joe DiMaggio never wanted to look ridiculous.

"DiMaggio was just as good in the field as he was at bat.

He played a very shallow center field and had the best throwing arm in baseball. You just didn't run on him. They say the greatest catch he ever made was on me. It was a ball I hit in Yankee Stadium about four hundred thirty or forty feet and he caught it behind the flagpole just in front of that fence that says 461 feet. He was playing me straight away, maybe three hundred feet from the plate and I got under the ball and hit this tremendous drive toward deep, straightaway center field. As I hit it I figure it's going to hit the wall and maybe I can get an inside-the-park home run on it. See, I'm always thinking of those RBIs. Earl Averill was on first and he takes off for second and I'm running to first. I look up and I see DiMaggio going back on the ball; it's still in the air and he's still chasing it. All of a sudden he sort of curls behind that flagpole and those monuments out there, sticks up his glove, and he's got the baseball. He was as shocked about catching the ball as I was. Averill hustled back toward first base and DiMaggio just sort of trotted in toward the infield with the ball. He forgot there was only one out when he caught the ball. It was just about the only time I ever saw him make a mistake. I was glad it happened. Just proved he was human.

"I don't think I ever said anything to DiMaggio about the catch until years later. He just wasn't the kind of guy you would stop and chat with as you crossed in the field or as he came to first base. I don't think I have had dinner with Joe DiMaggio alone in my life. We've been at a lot of banquets together and baseball affairs, but never just Joe and I. Players didn't socialize much in those days, even with their own teammates. Everybody had his own friends off the field. About the only guys I ever went out with were Jo-Jo White, who was my roommate, and Fred Hutchinson later on, and Billy Sullivan, and another Jewish kid pitcher from Brooklyn, Harry Eisenstat."

Greenberg—who suffered so much abuse as the American League's great Jewish star—was the first opposing player to talk to Jackie Robinson when Robinson, the first Negro player, entered baseball in 1947. Traded to Pittsburgh for his final season, Greenberg made a public show of cordiality for Robinson in the first game between the Dodgers and the Pirates.

"There weren't too many Jewish players in the league then, and there would be guys that would really ride us. I was young and I was sensitive when they called me 'Hey, Heeb' or 'Jewboy' or 'Sheeny Jew' or something like that. I realized after a while that that was the way it was. They talked like that to everybody. Guys on our club would yell at DiMaggio, 'Hey, Dago,' 'Hey, Big Wop,' 'Hey, you Big Guinea,' and things like that. One guy always called DiMaggio 'Spaghetti Bender' and Joe would never move. The pitchers were the worst ones. On the days they weren't pitching they'd have nothing to do so they would get on everybody. Joe never looked at them. Williams would go nuts. They used to needle him about being so skinny or about how fidgety he was at the plate. He'd start yelling back at them. DiMaggio never gave any of the bench jockeys any satisfaction. He was no Ted Williams. The funniest thing about all this name calling was how harmless it really was. Years later, when I was the general manager at Cleveland and Chicago, the guys who had called me the most names when I played wanted to be my best friends. Those are the guys who would always call me and ask me for coaching jobs or scouting jobs or managerial jobs in our system. If they thought I felt uneasy about the names, they never would have called.

"Joe never seemed to take note of anything anybody else did or said. He just did his own job. I think I can remember only one time when he said something that proved to be a mistake. I used to hit Johnny Murphy, the old Yankee relief pitcher, very hard. I was four-for-four against him

76

the first game I faced him. Then every other time I faced him throughout his career I really murdered him. I had a lot of home runs and RBIs against him. The reason was that I was a guess hitter. Murphy was a curve-ball pitcher. If I knew when his curve was coming I could kill it. I could hit anybody if I knew where the pitch was coming from. One time he strikes me out with a sidearm curve in Yankee Stadium. Then I face him the next time in Detroit, the count is three and two, and I know he will throw me that sidearm curve again. I hit it in the upper deck. He usually threw curves to me and wasted the fast ball. The next time I face him he walks by DiMaggio in center field, stops, and they talk. Later on I find out DiMaggio said to him, 'He's always looking for your curve. Why don't you give him your fast ball?' Now he comes to the mound. I'm still looking for that curve ball. That's his best pitch. All of a sudden here comes a fast ball. It's not so fast and I'm so anxious to hit it that I get under it and foul it off. Now he throws three curves in a row—one is a strike and two are called balls. The count is two and two, and I step out of the box for a second and think about it. He had talked to DiMaggio in center field and DiMaggio knew I always hit his curve. I decided DiMaggio had suggested the fast ball. This time I'm thinking fast ball and it comes in like a grapefruit—Murphy's fast ball wasn't very fast—and I hit it over the roof. I think after that DiMaggio let Murphy pitch and Murphy let DiMaggio play center field.

"In later years we talked about that a few times. I would see Joe every so often in Toots Shor's. I would play some tennis with Billy Talbert or Vic Seixas, and then I would go over to Shor's for lunch. DiMaggio would be sitting there with Shor, and Toots would call me over and we'd have a drink together. Joe would be getting ready to go some place and Toots would be telling him, 'Don't go yet, Joe. Have another beer.' Toots was very possessive of Joe. He wanted to keep him around and he wanted to keep him to himself.

"People would always be looking over at DiMaggio and trying to get his autograph. It's not easy being Joe Di-Maggio. I remember when I was playing—and it was before television—and people would recognize you. Now they recognize everybody because of television, but in those days only the big stars had that problem. You couldn't go to a restaurant on the road without some jerk coming over and wanting to talk about the game. Sometimes you were oh-for-four and you just didn't want to talk about the game. Fans always think they know you personally because they watch the game or read about you in the papers. Sometimes you just didn't feel like being gracious, but they were John Q. Public and they paid the freight, and they felt they owned you. Any time you ever read a story about a fan and a player getting into a scuffle, it can't ever be the player's fault. No player ever went up to a fan in a restaurant and started a conversation.

"There were times when I was playing when I'd come out of the gate—DiMaggio never went through this because he wouldn't leave the clubhouse until all the fans were gone—and there would be a hundred kids out there and you'd sign a few autographs before you jumped in a cab or got in a car. Maybe you wouldn't get all of them, and if you said you had to go there would be one kid with a pen who would shake his pen with ink—that was before ball points—and it would get all over your suit. I had a lot of good suits ruined by fans outside ball parks.

"I see Joe once in a while now at some dinner like the New York baseball writers' dinner or that big thing we had in Washington in 1969 or some charity affair. He's always friendly, always affable, but Joe is a hard guy to make conversation with. I used to go down to the old Biltmore Baths and sit around for a couple of hours. Joe used to go there a lot too. But we never ran into each other. I would come in and they would tell me Joe had just left or I would hear the next day that he had come in five minutes after I left. I always wondered what it would be like if we ever sat in the Turkish bath together for two or three hours. I wondered if he would talk a lot in the bath.

"I guess I know Joe almost forty years now. We've played hundreds of games against each other. I've talked to him hundreds of times at banquets and at Shor's and places like that. In a way, though, I guess I really don't know him. I don't know if anybody knows Joe DiMaggio."

In baseball 1936 was an important year. It was the year Joe DiMaggio joined the Yankees. It was also the year Robert William Andrew Feller joined the Cleveland Indians. Some people consider him the best pitcher of all time.

Bobby Feller was born on a farm in Van Meter, Iowa. He spurned farm chores for baseball and at fifteen was the talk of the territory as a young right-handed pitcher who could throw harder than any man alive. "Rapid Robert" was signed by the Indians upon graduation from high school and joined them as a seventeen-year-old with no professional experience. He was a regular starter at eighteen and considered the best pitcher in baseball before he was twenty. In 1939, before his twenty-first birthday, he won twenty-four games and lost only nine.

Feller became one of baseball's great drawing cards, a pitcher who could not only pack his home stadium but do the same in seven other cities around the league. Strikeouts were his trademark. With his incredible fast ball and exploding curve ball, Feller established numerous records. On October 2, 1938, pitching against Detroit, he became the first man to strike out eighteen batters in a nine-inning game. He ended Greenberg's chance to catch Babe Ruth's sixty-homer record that day and struck out one man, outfielder Chet Laabs, five times. He went on to establish a season record of 348 strikeouts in 1946. His pitching style and high kick were an awesome sight. The excitement of this man, Bob Feller, pitching against Joe DiMaggio has never been matched in baseball.

"Joe was the toughest right-handed batter I ever faced. He seemed always able to get that crucial hit in the late innings any time he wanted. He didn't have that quickness at bat that Ted had or Yogi Berra later on, but he didn't need it. He had such great strength. He could just over-power the best fast ball I could throw to him.

"When I was a kid I had two separate fast balls I threw to Joe. One had this big hop and rose up and in on him. The other jumped away from him. He hit them both.

"I guess if it's any consolation—but not much—Joe never hit those huge home runs off me like Greenberg or Williams did. Joe hit them far enough, though. I think in the early years he didn't pull as many balls on me as he did later. He was a line-drive hitter, and if I really had a good fast ball he would hit it to right field or right center.

"I don't know what the records show, but I guess Joe hit me better than anybody around. You couldn't fool him. One time, after he hit my curve and my fast ball, Rollie Hemsley, my catcher, figured we might catch him over-swinging if we gave him a changeup. So we set him up with a fast ball off the plate and then we came back with the change. He hit that damn thing into the upper deck too. That was it with the change. If he was going to hit me, he would have to hit my best fast ball and best curve.

"I really did enjoy the confrontations with him. He hit me good, sure, but I got him plenty of times too. That's the way it worked. You sort of remember the times a hitter gets you and not the times you get him. He seemed to hit the ball hard four out of five times off me. I was always trying

80

to get him to hit the ball on the ground and he was always trying to get it in the air and knock it off a wall some place.

"I think after a while the fans and the sportswriters made more of a rivalry out of it than Joe and I did. I had to get out a lot of other good hitters to beat the Yankees, and he couldn't beat me by himself very often either. It got so it was more or less like a circus when we faced each other. It was a good show and the fans got excited. I don't think I thought too much about it during the game. I was always concentrating on getting everybody out, not just Joe. I don't think I tried harder to get Joe out than I tried to get anybody alse out. It just seemed harder to get him out because he was a better hitter than anybody else.

"I don't think Joe and I could have ever been considered good friends. I would see him at these baseball clambakes, and we would say hello and that would be about it. He had his friends and I had my friends and we didn't get together and talk about the rivalry. There would always be a lot of fans around him and a lot of fans around me, so we couldn't have too many private chats even if we wanted to.

"That's one of the things about being a baseball star. There always are well-wishers around ready to buy you a steak. I didn't need that. I could afford to buy my own steak. I made it a point not to be too friendly with fans anyway.

"When I got older and pitching got a little harder, I had to concentrate even more. That's one of the reasons I wanted to concentrate only on the hitters and not on what some reporter wanted to know. I guess it's easier with a regular. He's in there every day and he learns to take the good days with the bad. When a pitcher has a bad day he has to wait three or four days to come back. That's when pitching is really tough—when you are having a couple of bad games and you have to wait out your next start.

81

"That's why I used to enjoy the train rides in the old days. You'd get in the car and gather around with a lot of the guys and talk about the last game or the next game and work on some things you could do to help your ball club. We used to talk over strategy and how to handle some guys and some teams and try to search out weaknesses and strengths of all the different guys. I don't think we ever had much luck coming up with a weakness on DiMaggio. I guess he just never had any weakness.

"In our day you did most of your talking with your own teammates. Now there is a lot of hobnobbing with the players on the other teams—they go out together; they talk on the field, around the hotels, all over. That never happened when I played. If a guy was on another club he was an enemy. That was all there was to it. There were guys you played with on the All-Star team and they would never even say hello. You knew the next day they would be trying to beat you and you would be trying to beat them, so what was the sense of being buddy-buddy?

"I probably talk more to Joe now when I see him at one of these baseball things than I ever did when we were playing. He really seems to enjoy talking about golf, and I think he has worked on his golf game the way he worked on his hitting. Joe was like that as a ballplayer. He was always trying to improve himself. That's the way it should be. Some guys were like that.

"When I think back to those days when everybody was talking about the rivalry, I guess I didn't realize part of it was to build up interest in me and DiMaggio so we could excite the fans when the Yankees came into town and sell out the stadium. We sure did draw some people, all right, and it was an exciting time. I have to admit that. I wanted to beat everybody, but the Yankees were on top so I probably did enjoy beating them the most.

"Believe me, it was fun when I went against DiMaggio

and the park was jammed and everybody was screaming. It was the most fun, yes, sir, when I could bust the fast ball by him."

Jim Hegan, the catcher for the Indians, was the man crouched down behind DiMaggio in many of those contests with Feller. Early in 1974, at the spring-training camp of the Detroit Tigers at Lakeland, Florida, Coach Jim Hegan leaned against an outfield fence and talked about Joe.

"He would come to the plate, dig in, pump his bat once, and stand there. He was ready. He wasn't like Williams. Ted was fidgety at the plate; he would always be high. Ted always got up for Feller and later on he got up for Herb Score. You could see the determination he had against the very good ones. DiMaggio never did that. He got ready at the plate exactly the same way for every pitcher. Feller had a great deal of emotion and excitement about him when he was facing DiMaggio. DiMaggio never showed any of that against Feller. You couldn't tell if he was facing Feller or if he was facing some kid up from the minors five minutes ago.

"DiMaggio was a great curve-ball hitter. Feller was known for his speed but he had this fantastic curve. The ball would come right at a right-handed hitter's head, then start breaking and wind up at the knees for a strike. Most of them moved away from it. Not DiMaggio. He just stood there at the plate, watched it break, and then hit it hard some place. Feller tried everything against him—high, low, inside, outside, curve, fast ball. Nothing helped. He just could hit everything Bob threw up to the plate.

"DiMaggio could always take a close pitch in a tough situation because the umpires would give it to him. I can't ever remember DiMaggio or Williams being called out on a three-two pitch. The umpires figured those guys knew the strike zone better than they did. If it was going to be a pitch they would take, the umpires would call it a ball. I guess the umpires felt the fans came to see Joe and Ted hit. They didn't want them struck out without a swing. Why it was all right to walk them without a swing and it wasn't all right to strike them out without a swing I never could figure.

"I guess I was in the league five years or so before Joe said hello to me. That's just the way he was. One day he walked up to the plate, said hello, and I almost fell through a hole in the ground. He just wasn't an emotional or talkative guy. He did all his talking with his bat and glove.

"Williams had this habit of coming up to the plate when a guy was warming up, and I used to kid him about it. He would be sneaking up and I would tell him the next one will get him in the kneecap. He would laugh. You didn't do that with DiMaggio. He didn't sneak up to the plate, and when he got there it was business. He didn't kid at the plate and you didn't kid him.

"Joe didn't have a weakness in the game. He did everything well. I think Williams was probably a little better hitter, stronger for sure, and maybe a little quicker with the bat. But Joe was the best all-around ballplayer I've ever seen. Williams was a great defensive player at Fenway. He could play that wall and hold doubles to singles with a quick relay. Outside of Fenway he was nothing special. DiMaggio was special all over, at Yankee Stadium or on the road. He could catch the ball anywhere, hit any pitch, steal a base if he needed to, stretch a hit, do whatever had to be done to help the Yankees win a ball game. He was just a complete ballplayer. I've been in the game more than thirty years now. I've never seen anybody do as many things well as Joe could. He was by himself."

Because of the strange mechanics of hitting a baseball,

every batter has one pitcher who bothers him more than any other. It could be the way the man throws the ball or the way his pitch moves that destroys a batter's timing. Or simply a mental block. A pitcher retires a hitter easily the first time they meet and the hitter is on the defensive forever after until he learns to *hit* the pitcher. Sometimes he never does. Bobby Feller was the best pitcher in the American League and Joe DiMaggio hit him hard and regularly.

DiMaggio almost never hit a pitcher named Melvin LeRoy Harder. Mel Harder grew up in Nebraska and was signed by the independent Omaha club as a seventeen-year-old right-hander in 1927. He was sold to the Cleveland Indians in 1928 and played for them from 1928 through 1947. He had an excellent curve ball, was a very smart pitcher, and had great skill in keeping the hitters off balance with his mixture of speed and stuff.

Mel Harder was the one pitcher who had Joe DiMaggio's number and the one pitcher DiMaggio hated to confront.

"I've heard Joe say that I was the toughest pitcher he ever faced and I was always flattered by that. It was always kind to be remembered and it certainly was a thrill to be remembered even a little bit as a guy who gave the great DiMaggio any trouble out there. Joe and I always got along fine off the field. We'd say hello to each other and that was about all each of us wanted to say. I was always on the quiet side myself. There really wasn't that much to say on a ball field. If you are concentrating on the game, you are too busy thinking about the hitters or Joe about the pitcher to get into too much chitchat.

"I used to get Joe out mostly with the good sinker I threw. He wouldn't get a good piece of the ball and he would beat it down into the dirt. I threw a lot of different pitches. That's probably why I gave Joe so much trouble. I had a good sinker, good fast ball, good curve ball, and good

85

change, and I could spot it. I think he was always looking for the wrong pitch. I was always trying to set him up to hit the sinker, so I would throw the curve ball out of the strike zone. Then I might come back with a sinker down and just off the plate and he would be a little off the pitch and not get a good rip. The sinker was always a tough pitch to hit and it was very tough for those sluggers who wanted to uppercut the ball and get it in the air. He had a compact swing but he sometimes had trouble with the sinker when I got it on the outside corner. There are just some pitches that are difficult to hit, no matter who the hitter is.

"I never tried to pitch Joe in any pattern. I would pitch him according to the count and not according to what I got him out on last time.

"I guess I made my reputation against Joe in one game in Cleveland. I don't remember what year it was but it probably was 1941 or 1942 because we were playing them before a big crowd and it was at night. I struck Joe out three times and popped him up. I just had great stuff that night and outguessed Joe every time. I should have gotten a medal for striking Joe DiMaggio out three times in one night. Sometimes I didn't strike him out three times in one season.

"I handled Joe pretty well in my career, but there were plenty of guys who wore me out. Probably the two toughest guys for me were Charlie Gehringer and Lou Gehrig. I had pretty good success against Ruth and Williams but Gehringer wore me out. He would foul off a lot of good pitches and then I would miss by an inch or so and he would get a piece of the ball and drop it into left field. Gehrig was just a good hitter. He could pull the inside pitch into the seats at Yankee Stadium or he could drive a ball hard to left field. I think he hit it harder to left field than any left-handed hitter in the game. He was strong enough to hit the sinker hard to every field. Hitting is a mental thing anyway. Sometimes I would outguess them and sometimes they would outguess me.

"When I think about it I really don't know why Joe didn't do better against me. Maybe I got him out the first time I faced him and he couldn't believe it. He probably figured he should be creaming me with that stuff I had, especially at the end, when I couldn't throw hard any more. I don't know really. I guess I'm just grateful I had good luck against him. It kept me around for a long time."

8: Class

To date, the Yankees have won twenty-nine pennants and twenty world championships, a record of success unequaled in professional baseball. On the face of it, DiMaggio's Yankees (1936–1951) contributed more to that record than Ruth's (1920–1934). Ruth played on seven pennant winners and four world championship teams during his fourteen years with New York. DiMaggio played on ten pennant winners and nine world-championship teams in his thirteen seasons. The question of which generation of Yankees was better, however, is one that is still debated. One thing was sure: to most people, betting against the Yankees, was like betting against U.S. Steel. A favorite cry was: "Break up the Yankees!"

Along with DiMaggio, the second Yankee dynasty included men like Gordon, Keller, Henrich, Ruffing, Rizzuto, and Dickey.

Bill Dickey today is still the same courtly Southern gentleman he was when he first came out of Little Rock, Arkansas, in 1928 to join the team. He was a durable left-handed power hitter, had a fine throwing arm, and was considered as bright a catcher as ever played the game. His best friend was Lou Gehrig.

"Lou was a wonderful fellow, a gentleman at all times, a really remarkable man. He loved kids. He would stand against the rail at the stadium and talk to them all the time. He drank very little, and he really took care of himself. He could be moody at times and very quiet. Then he would snap out of it and laugh easily. He was a streak hitter. He'd go for days hitting line drive after line drive. Then suddenly he would stop, for no reason. He worried a lot about his hitting. He always had to be reassured. He could probably hit a ball harder in every direction than any man who ever played. Lou could hit hard line drives past an outfielder the way I hit hard line drives past an infielder.

"I really don't like to talk about the relationship between Ruth and Gehrig. It just is unpleasant to think about even now. When I went up there they were good friends and they kidded each other a lot and they got along fine. Then something happened. I don't want to tell you about it. They were never friends again. You know that famous picture of Babe hugging Lou when Lou had that retirement ceremony at the stadium in 1939? Well, Babe put his arms around Lou and hugged him but, if you look close, Lou never put his arm around the Babe. Lou just never forgave him."

The bitterness between Ruth and Gehrig developed in their last years together. Gehrig had been courting a beautiful woman. Somehow Ruth met the woman and turned on the charm, and the woman dropped Gehrig. It was a bitter blow to Gehrig, a sensitive and insecure man.

"I remember when DiMaggio joined our club in '36. He was the all-around perfect player. I think his record speaks for itself. We won the pennant seven out of eight years after he joined us. I had only been on one winner before that, in '32. Lou and Joe got along fine but they didn't socialize.

Lou didn't resent the attention Joe got. Lou just went out and did his job every day. There were times Lou would come over to me and apologize because he thought he had hurt my feelings by not talking for a couple of days. He worried about other people's feelings. Joe and Lou were alike in one way. They both seemed dedicated and concerned with the game.

"It's funny to think about it now, but I think DiMaggio was underestimated as a player. He did things so easily, people didn't realize how good he was. DiMaggio would hit a home run but nobody would get excited. He never hit those towering home runs, not like the kind Ruth hit or Gehrig hit, or Ralph Kiner later on. Joe's would just be nice line drives, a few rows back, enough to count but not enough to make you realize he had put another one in there.

"DiMaggio made our club. He could do so many things to keep the other team from beating you. Nobody in baseball could come in on a line drive like Joe, and he could throw the ball on a dime. One time we were playing a game after a heavy rain. Somebody hit a line single to center with a man on second. The grass was very wet and I didn't think Joe would attempt a throw home. Well, he gets the ball and he lets it go. He used to throw the ball perfectly on a big bounce. This time he realized the ground was wet so he didn't want to take a chance on a bad bounce. He threw it on a fly—like a line drive, really. I was down because I thought he would throw on a bounce like he always did and low so I could make the tag. Well, the ball came in a *perfect* line from center field. I just wasn't thinking. It was shoulder high but I never went up for it. The ball sailed over my head and hit the stands behind the plate on one big bounce. If I had caught it the runner would have been out by fifteen feet.

"I caught a little in '46 after I got out of the service, but my knees used to shake a lot so I knew I had to quit."

Then a large, hulking young man, Charles "Red" Ruffing could both pitch and hit. Signed by the Red Sox at the age of seventeen, Ruffing did not have a single winning season with them in six years and actually led the league in losses for two consecutive seasons. Then, in 1930, the Yankees purchased his contract for fifty thousand dollars, and it all changed for Ruffing. He had fourteen winning seasons in the next fifteen years, including four twenty-game years in a row.

"I guess I played with the three best hitters of all time in Ruth, Gehrig, and DiMaggio.

"Joe kind of proved himself in that first spring training. He hit some balls hard and made those easy catches and you knew he could play. After that it just seemed a question of him staying healthy.

"I played a lot of years so I can't say what our best ball club was but I know we were better after DiMaggio joined us than we were before. There's no question about that.

"It was just nice to turn around and watch him out there in center field. You saw him standing out there and you knew you had a pretty damn good chance to win the baseball game."

Joe Gordon joined the Yankees in 1938 and played seven years with them as a smooth-fielding second baseman and home-run-hitting batter. He hit 30 home runs in 1940 and 253 in his eleven-year career.

"Joe wasn't a mixer on the club. He stayed by himself. Now they all stay by themselves. They carry those goddamn briefcases and run out to see their brokers as soon as they hit a town. We used to stand around the hotel lobby and talk baseball. I roomed with Red Rolfe and when we got into a town we put our bags in the room and got right back down to the lobby. You had to. The rooms were so goddamn hot. They didn't have any air conditioning in those days, and if you opened the window in July and August in St. Louis or Chicago or some place, you got nothing in there but some more hot air. Rolfe and I used to figure the lobby was the coolest place, out of the sun and with a little breeze from the people going in and out. A lot of those places had revolving doors, and that would keep the air moving. We used to go in and out of those doors just to get some cool air.

"We traveled by train and things were a lot slower. No air conditioning on the trains either. We played a lot of bridge, about a twentieth of a penny a point. Gehrig was a good bridge player and he and Dickey played together a lot. Then Selkirk and Myril Hoag played with them. I got in the games once in a while. I wasn't very good. They just took me along for the ride.

"DiMaggio was already the star when I got there in '38. He was the best hitter I ever saw. He could hit the best pitches from the best pitchers—you know, those damn curves falling off a table, or that fast ball low and on the outside part of the plate. Hell, he'd just wait on it and whack the damn thing into right center for a triple. He was an easy guy to get along with. He didn't make any fuss. Didn't ask for any privileges. Just got into his uniform and did his work. I think he got along with everybody except Larry MacPhail. MacPhail took over the club, and I think DiMaggio thought MacPhail was rocking the boat with all the fuss he made.

"I wasn't mad at Joe when I heard he had something to do with the trade to Cleveland. Hell, I had some good years there and won a pennant. They were going to trade me anyway; it was just a question of which pitcher they wanted. The '46 season was a bad year.

"Those Yankee teams were great, but we didn't all get rich playing for them. They used to give you that crap about how much extra money you would make for winning the World Series. Then they would give you less salary, like that was part of your salary. I thought that was pretty awful. I had to hold out my first year with the Yankees to get up to five thousand dollars. Then I got a fifteen-hundred-dollar raise the next year after we won the pennant. I got up to eleven thousand dollars after five years. Things were better with the Indians. I was making thirty-five thousand dollars when I quit.

"DiMaggio was so good and we had so many other good players that we dominated the league when I was there. That can't happen any more. The players are spread out too thin. Clubs are more balanced now. Everything's different. There's more income from television so the players are all making big money. They don't need that World Series money like we did.

"When I think about DiMaggio I guess the hitting streak has to be the most impressive thing, but I wish I had some records of the runs he drove in for us in games after the seventh, eighth, and ninth innings. The great players can do that. They can be having a bad day, maybe oh-for-two or oh-for-three, and now the game is hanging and it's the ninth inning and the same pitcher that's been getting a guy out easily all day can't do it any more. He was like that in the streak too. I bet he got a lot of those hits the last time up. Joe just hit the ball harder and more consistently than anybody I ever saw.

"He was a guy who just liked to be by himself. Why, I remember when I first came to the Yankees in '38 and I got married and lived in the Grand Concourse Hotel in the Bronx, right down from the stadium. There'd be six or eight couples living in that hotel, and the guys would walk to the ball park together and the women would sit around and talk and do the dishes and come on over later. Now the players all live far away in the suburbs and they never see each other except in the clubhouse and on the field. They play the game and then they scatter like quail."

Tommy Henrich was the right fielder. He was a left-handed hitter and a left-handed-throwing outfielder and first baseman from the football town of Massillon, Ohio. The Yankees signed him for twenty thousand dollars and a twenty-thousand-dollar salary. As a clutch batter, he earned the nickname of Old Reliable for the way he broke up games with big hits in the late innings.

"Old Reliable, I always got a kick out of that. Russ Hodges, the broadcaster, gave that one to me. We were playing a game against the Athletics at the stadium and were leaving after the game to make a train and go on a Western trip. We were ahead by a run in the ninth inning. We had two out and Buddy Rosar was up. He hit a popup right behind the plate. Ken Silvestri missed it. As those things happen, Rosar hit the next pitch into the seats and we were all tied up. Now it looks like we are going to blow our train. Rizzuto leads off the bottom of the ninth and hits a triple. Now the winning run is on third, time is getting close for making the train, and I'm up. I hit the first pitch up the alley in right center field and we win the game. Hodges is on the air and he's yelling, 'Henrich did it again, Old Reliable that he is, and the Yankees will make the train.' After that they started calling me Old Reliable.

"It's funny that I ever became a baseball player at all. I never even thought about it as a kid. When I was in high school I never played hardball. I was a softball player. I played right field and shortstop. I was playing for Huffman Drugs in town. We won eighty games one year and lost seven. This guy used to give us two hundred dollars for our team. We bought uniforms, gloves, balls, bats, the whole works out of that. This one year they had a bazaar in town. Just after we got our two hundred dollars this bazaar opened up. Well, instead of buying our gloves and bats and balls we all went to this bazaar. We lost the two hundred dollars. The team broke up after that. A few days later some guy in town who had a semipro baseball team asked me if I wanted to play for him. I was just a kid and he was going to pay me five bucks a game so I took it. Then Cleveland signed me." Then the Yanks.

"The only thing that I don't like about baseball now is the Little League program: the kids get to play a couple of innings and that's it. When I was a kid I used to play ball all day. I remember once when I joined the Yankees and Joe Gordon and I were talking about the best day we ever had as kid players. I told him I once had fifty hits in a day. It wasn't unusual. When you start playing at eight in the morning and you don't stop until eight at night, you get a chance for fifty hits. I think my best day was fifty-for-fifty-six or something like that.

"Well, anyway, I signed with the Yankees. Here's something I never told anybody. I lied about my age. The Yankees thought I was eighteen when they signed me. Hell, I was twenty-one. That's why I quit instead of having that knee operation. I was already thirty-eight. They thought I was thirty-five and had a few more years. I knew I was finished even if I did have the operation.

"I got to the Yankees and I saw DiMaggio play a few games and I realized in a hurry this was the greatest player I had ever seen. It didn't take long to recognize that kind of talent. Just say he was the greatest ballplayer I ever saw in my life, the greatest ballplayer any of us ever saw, and let it go at that.

"Joe was kind of a cold guy; everybody knows that. He never asked me out to dinner alone in all the years I was with the Yankees, but I never asked him either. It just seemed that we went our separate ways. There was never anything wrong between us. I never had a cross word with Joe. We would ride in a cab to the ball park together or dress next to each other or sit down together on the train, but we never really kidded around a lot. Joe just wasn't the type you kidded around with. He roomed with Gomez, and Gomez was the only person I ever saw who could kid DiMaggio in front of other people and get away with it. Lefty would make fun of him or call him a silly name and Joe would just laugh. Nobody else could get away with that. Nobody else would try.

"Joe had a lot of character. He was the most moral man I ever knew. He couldn't do anything cheap; he wouldn't do anything that would hurt his name or hurt the Yankees. He really felt an obligation to the public, to the fans, and to the club. If you needed a favor he would do it without a fuss.

"I think DiMaggio felt bad when I told him I was quitting. We had been together a long time and now it was over. He didn't say much but I knew he felt it. You get pretty close on a baseball team when you go through a lot of pennant fights, even if you are not talking about everything in the world every day."

Charlie Keller is small, not heavy, his hair still black and thick, his menacing, bushy eyebrows now flecked with gray. His voice is soft. He is the man who was considered the physically strongest person in baseball, whose very appearance would intimidate a pitcher and who was unmercifully kidded about his nickname—King Kong. Keller joined the Yankees in 1939 and played left field with verve for ten seasons. Then he had a serious back operation, was traded away, and came back for a short time before retiring in 1952.

"When I came to the Yankees I think everyone recognized that Joe was already the best player in the game. There was no question that he was the greatest player I've ever seen. I'll only hedge this much—maybe Ted Williams was a better hitter. Maybe. There was one thing about Joe that nobody ever came close to. That was the kind of competitor he was, how he took responsibility for winning or losing, how he got the big hits in the big spots. You ask if the guys looked to DiMaggio to win a game. No. It wasn't that. It makes good reading how everybody depended on him, but that's not how it was. Everybody went out and did his own job and that's why we won. DiMaggio was the best player, but everybody had to contribute for us to win.

"Joe and I never really went around together. We'd have an occasional beer and a sandwich after a game or something like that, but he went his way and I went mine most of the time. Joe liked to go to the movies a lot. I hated movies. I would spend a lot of time reading and listening to the radio on those off days when Joe was in the movies. The relationship with Joe and the other guys wasn't close. I couldn't say that. But he was a solid guy, and if anybody needed help or advice or anything like that Joe was there. We spent a lot of time on the train and there were bridge games going most of the time. I played once in a while. Dickey and Rolfe were in most of the games. Joe watched once in a while.

"Joe was hurt a lot. There were a lot of days when he shouldn't have been out there and he was. You had to respect him for that. He would be in that training room getting taped up or swallowing some pills to kill the pain, and we wouldn't know if he was playing or not. All of a sudden he would be on the lineup card and on the field like nothing was wrong.

"You get old in baseball and you start getting injuries. It happens to everybody—some a little earlier than others. When you are a kid you don't get hurt as much and, if you do, you shake it off quickly. When you are older the little hurts become big ones and they stay around a lot longer."

Pete Sheehy knew them all. He became the clubhouse man for the Yankees in 1927. He still is.

"I can describe Joe in one word: class. He was the most perfect ballplayer I ever saw. Joe was a shy fellow but he loosened up. He would come in early and stay late. Ruth used to stay late. Not Gehrig. He'd be the first one dressed and on home to his momma. DiMaggio would sit down at his locker and say, 'Pete, half a cup of coffee.' Never a full cup. Just half a cup. He must have drunk thirty half-a-cups of coffee a day. Funny, now he doesn't touch coffee. Just tea. He used to smoke a lot too. Joe was a nervous sort. It was all inside him. He was intense. He would smoke a pack of Camels every day before the game. Sometimes during the game he would sneak under the stands and have a smoke in between innings. Now I think he's stopped smoking.

"He wasn't no problem. He didn't ask for special favors. He wore regular-size clothes: 44 shirt, 36 pants. They weren't made to order and tapered like they are now. He always looked good in his unform—in his street clothes too. We were good friends. He invited me to his wedding when he married Dorothy Arnold in San Francisco. I met Marilyn a couple of times too. She seemed like a very nice girl. Now sometimes before Old Timers' Day he calls me up and asks me to get him a pair of shoes or something he might need. I always get what he wants. Joe always took good care of me, a real good tipper. I look forward to seeing him every year at Old Timers' Day. It seems like all the players do. When he comes into the clubhouse they all jump up and greet him, 'Hi ya, Joe. How you doin', Joe?' and like that. He seems to enjoy it. I'll tell you something else. When Joe DiMaggio walks into the clubhouse, the lights flicker. He's the star."

97

9: The Streak

It all began in Yankee Stadium on May 15, 1941. The Yankees had lost the pennant the year before, the first time they had lost it since DiMaggio joined the team, and this year they were barely holding their own with fourteen wins and fourteen losses. The team wasn't hitting much, and DiMaggio's own average had dropped to .304; he had had only nine hits in his last thirty-nine times at bat. For the past two days he hadn't gotten any hits at all, going oh-for-three against Bobby Feller and oh-for-four against his nemesis, Mel Harder.

On that cool Thursday afternoon, in a game against Chicago, rookie Phil Rizzuto began the bottom of the first inning with a double. Red Rolfe and Charlie Keller flied out. DiMaggio, batting fourth, lined a single to left field against a crafty curve-balling left-hander named Edgar Smith.

Every day for the next ten days DiMaggio got at least one hit. In the eleventh game he got *four* hits, including a home run. And on he went.

On June 5 he hit a triple off a young Detroit southpaw named Hal Newhouser. A streak was now becoming apparent. Hitting in up to twenty consecutive games is relatively common for good batters. Anything over twenty is unusual. The National League hitting record was thirty-three straight games, achieved by Rogers Hornsby; the American League record was George Sisler's forty-one.

As the DiMaggio streak passed twenty games, the sports pages began acknowledging it. With games number twenty-five, twenty-six, and twenty-seven, reports of DiMaggio's hitting status moved toward the top of the columns. As he closed on Hornsby's record, he got top billing. As he matched Hornsby's achievement, Joe DiMaggio's streak became a national passion.

The smallest incident suddenly took on a major significance. As DiMaggio jogged in after a game one day, a youngster ran out onto the field and grabbed his cap. Joe retrieved it quickly. "It's not the cap," Joe DiMaggio explained to writer Tom Meany. "It's the kids sticking their fingers in your eyes, down your neck, on your forehead. Anything can happen when they do that." Like most players, he also saw the loss of a familiar, comfortable cap as a possible disturbance to his equilibrium and performance.

On June 21 DiMaggio hit a single off Detroit right-hander Paul "Dizzy" Trout. The streak was at thirty-four games. He had passed Hornsby and was moving on George Sisler.

"That's when the pressure really started," DiMaggio said later. "That's when the public, the press, and the pitchers really started noticing."

The rival league's pitchers watched the streak with a feigned lack of interest. Whitlow Wyatt, a Brooklyn Dodger pitcher, said he was surprised the streak had gone as far as it had. "Were Joe DiMaggio batting in our league, he would have to do most of his hitting from a sitting position. The pitching boys in this loop don't fool," Wyatt boasted. "They really knock a fellow down."

As for American League pitchers, they wanted to stop DiMaggio but never went out of their way to do it. Only one pitcher, Johnny Babich of the Philadelphia Athletics, showed much anger at what DiMaggio was doing to the art of pitching. Babich vowed he would end the streak. "I'll get him out the first time," said Babich, "and walk him the next three times. That'll stop him."

DiMaggio's teammates thought that would be rather unsporting and vowed to take vengeance on Babich if Joe was stopped by such a trick. DiMaggio made it all academic.

The next time he faced Babich, Joe hit the first pitch on a line, right between Babich's legs.

Hal Newhouser, the Detroit left-hander, pitched to Joe again on June 22—game number thirty-five. "The idea," Newhouser recalled, "was to make him hit a bad ball if you could. It was a challenge. When the streak really got going, everybody wanted to stop him. It would have been a great honor. I wish I had."

The streak went on: thirty-six, thirty-seven, thirty-eight, thirty-nine, forty straight games. Then it was one game away, one game to tie Sisler's record.

The Yankees played a doubleheader in Washington on June 29. DiMaggio hit a single off Dutch Leonard. The crowd of thirty-one thousand exploded. As he came back to the dugout, Joe's teammates leaped on him to hug and congratulate the man who had done it—had equaled the all-time record for consecutive hits.

DiMaggio sat quietly in the clubhouse between the games of the doubleheader. He changed his shirt, sipped at some coffee, and lit up a Camel. Now he had to do it again in the second game to break the magic mark.

But even if he could, it would still not be over. The night before, an amazing story had come in on the wires from San Francisco. A reporter named Jack McDonald had discovered that an obscure record preceded Sisler's. In 1897 Wee Willie Keeler of Baltimore (who had come out of Brooklyn in 1892 at five feet, four and a half inches and one hundred and forty pounds to collect 2,962 hits) had hit in forty-four straight games. So the record DiMaggio thought he was challenging was not the ultimate record at all.

To make matters worse, during the pause between the two games that day someone had stolen Joe's favorite bat from the rack at the end of the dugout. A frantic search ensued. No two bats are exactly alike, and the fraction-of-an-ounce difference in weight as well as the subtle differences in smoothness, size, and feel could have been enough to throw DiMaggio off stride, who was even more fanatic about his bats than most. But he accepted the situation and went to the plate in the second game with another bat. He failed to get a hit the first time up, and also the second.

Tommy Henrich, who used the same model, offered his to Joe. DiMaggio refused and stayed with his own backup bat. He failed again. Now he would have just one more chance.

"Okay," DiMaggio said to Henrich, before his final trip to the plate. "Let me have your bat."

A right-handed relief pitcher named Red Anderson was on the mound for the Senators. He fired a fast ball close to DiMaggio, leaning him back. DiMaggio guessed that the pitcher would throw outside and off speed for the next one. He watched the windup, watched the ball zooming at him, waited, swung, and cracked a single into left field.

Forty-two.

The crowd erupted. All the Yankees jumped off the bench to applaud and cheer DiMaggio, now standing on first base.

The Yankees were off the next day. DiMaggio rested at home with his wife, Dorothy, who was pregnant at the time, and listened to the radio. Every news program blared out that Joe DiMaggio would go for the consecutive-game hitting record.

It had become the most important event in America. Each day after Joe D's hit of the afternoon, news of it spread almost instantly into the nation's homes, offices, factories, schools. Bandleader Les Brown even introduced a song celebrating the phenomenal Joe. It got a lot of play that summer.

He started baseball's famous streak,
That's got us all aglow.
He's just a man and not a freak—
Joltin' Joe DiMaggio.

He'll live in Baseball's Hall of Fame.
He got there blow by blow.
Our kids will tell their kids his name—
Joltin' Joe DiMaggio.

Coast to coast that's all you hear
Of Joe the one-man show.
He's glorified the horsehide sphere—
Joltin' Joe DiMaggio.

Letters poured into Yankee Stadium. Many of DiMaggio's teammates were becoming nervous wrecks from the tension. But for all the near hysteria surrounding him, DiMaggio managed to remain outwardly calm. No one could discern excitement or nervousness in his deportment. Years later DiMaggio explained, "I was able to control myself. That doesn't mean I wasn't dying inside."

Joe had a hit in each of the next two games against the Red Sox, and the following day in Boston he broke Wee Willie Keeler's obscure record with a home run off right-hander Dick Newsome.

Newspapers of the time recorded the popular reaction. In San Francisco the fishermen on the wharf heard the news in the early afternoon and celebrated with wine. In Chicago a big, burly Italian truck driver heard the announcement on his radio, leaned out of his window to tell a pretty girl passing by, and got a kiss blown to him for his news. In Denver the announcement of DiMaggio's hit was made at a public roller-skating rink and the kids there banged on the boards with their skates. In Cincinnati, in a summer high school history class, a poll was taken to name the greatest

American of all times. Abraham Lincoln finished third, George Washington second, and Joe DiMaggio first.

And the streak went on. Forty-six, forty-eight, fifty, fifty-two, fifty-four. Would it ever end? Fifty-five in Chicago against Edgar Smith, the same man against whom it had started. Fifty-six in Cleveland against Al Milnar. Then . . .

There are events that survive the passage of time, that stay alive in memory despite all subsequent experience. For millions July 17, 1941, has that special significance.

That night there were 67,468 people in the stands at Cleveland's Municipal Stadium. It was the largest night-baseball crowd ever. They had come to see Joe DiMaggio extend his amazing streak. At that point he had had 91 hits in 223 times at bat (average .408). He had hit 15 home runs, batted in 55 runs, scored 56 runs—and electrified the nation.

Al Smith, a left-hander, was the Cleveland pitcher. In the top of the first inning DiMaggio came to bat with the Yankees ahead 1–0. With the count at one ball and no strikes, Joe pulled an inside pitch sharply over third base on two big bounces. The crowd gasped as the third baseman, Ken Keltner, moved over the line, backhanded the ball, and threw DiMaggio out.

In the fourth DiMaggio walked.

In the seventh he hit another hot ground ball at third base. Again Keltner fielded the sizzler, straightened up, and threw DiMaggio out—by a step.

In the eighth inning the Yankees were ahead 4–1 and DiMaggio faced relief pitcher Jim Bagby, Jr. It was one out and runners on first and second. The count went to two balls and one strike. DiMaggio lashed out at an inside fast ball and drove it, on the ground, toward center field. Lou Boudreau moved quickly to his left from the shortstop position, got in front of the ball, smoothly handled a bad hop, underhanded the ball to second baseman Ray Mack, and watched as Mack threw hard to first, trying for a double play. Joe was out. The fans went wild. The streak was over.

But was it?

The score was 4–1 in the bottom of the ninth. Two Cleveland runners were on and nobody was out. Pinch hitter Larry Rosenthal tripled to the right center field wall. Two runs scored. Rosenthal was on third and nobody was out. Score: four to three. If Cleveland tied the game and sent it into extra innings, DiMaggio might bat again. Johnny Murphy, relieving Lefty Gomez as he so often did, faced first baseman Hal Trosky. Murphy threw a curve ball and Trosky grounded sharply to first baseman Johnny Sturm for the first out. Rosenthal held third. Now the batter was Clarence "Soup" Campbell. He hit back to the mound. Rosenthal broke from third for the plate. Murphy alertly threw home and Rosenthal was out as Campbell reached first base. The next hitter was Roy "Stormy" Weatherly. He hit the first pitch to Phil Rizzuto at shortstop. The rookie fielded it cleanly and threw to Sturm at first base. The game and the streak were history.

Out in center field DiMaggio put his head down and looked at the grass, then jogged toward the third-base dugout. Reaching it, he climbed down the steps, trotted up the dugout ramp, walked through the open door of the clubhouse to his locker, threw his glove on the shelf, pulled off his shirt, took a Camel from his pants pocket, lit the cigarette, and sat down. The Yankees had won but the locker room was quiet. They were waiting for DiMaggio. Would he react bitterly to the end of the streak, to Keltner's two great plays, to Boudreau's lucky reaction to a bad-hop grounder, to the pitches that Al Smith and Jim Bagby were fortunate enough to get him out on?

"Well," said Joe DiMaggio, loud enough for all his teammates to hear, "that's over."

The players relaxed. Some came up to congratulate him on his incredible feat. Others deliberately stayed away. DiMaggio sat quietly at his locker for a few moments, alone, knowing what the next minutes would hold. Soon the clubhouse doors opened and more than two dozen reporters went straight to Joe.

"I can't say I'm glad it's over," he said. "Of course, I wanted it to go on as long as it could." He was calm, polite, stoic as always, unemotional about the end of the streak. He gave most of the credit to Keltner for his brilliant fielding plays.

Ken Keltner remembers that night in Cleveland very clearly.

"Al Smith was pitching for us and we went over DiMaggio before the game. Smith didn't have a fast ball. He had that screw ball and he threw it a lot to right-handed hitters. They still called it 'the fadeaway' in those days. I knew DiMaggio would be able to pull him, so that's why I was playing so close to the line. I was back deep because DiMaggio wasn't bunting.

"We were just as excited that night about DiMaggio's streak as the Yankees were. We wanted to stop it. It would be a feather in our caps. DiMaggio was a hell of a hitter and he was hot. When a good hitter is hot he's a tough guy to handle. Both balls he hit to me were tough plays, almost in the same spot. The first ball was a little more over toward the foul line and I wasn't sure I would get him. I was playing real deep and I had to backhand it and straighten up and throw. I just beat him. The next one was hit just as hard but not as far to my right. I knew I'd have him if I made a good throw.

"The whole thing was exciting because it had been built up so, and the Yankees were always exciting to play against. They were the best and you always wanted to beat them. Ending the streak really didn't mean anything to me. We lost the ball game and I was just mad about that. I was still pretty sore when I walked out of the park. A lot of people were hanging around outside the gate waiting for DiMaggio. They booed me as I came out. They wanted the streak to go on forever.

"I've seen Joe a couple of times through the years. He's quite a guy. We went out a couple of times in New York afterward. Joe was a great ballplayer. That was some night. It's funny when I think about it. I played thirteen years in the game and I bet more people ask me about the night that DiMaggio was stopped than about anything else."

Ruth dominated 1927, Roger Maris dominated 1961, and Hank Aaron dominated 1974. Joe DiMaggio *ruled* 1941. Phil "Scooter" Rizzuto, then a rookie shortstop for the Yankees, spoke of that summer with awe.

"The 1941 streak was an unbelievable thing. Day after day after day. I don't think he got a soft hit the entire fifty-six games. When he broke George Sisler's record in Washington we almost pounded him into a broken back. There were so many great games in the streak. I guess I remember best the hit he got off Johnny Babich of Philadelphia. Babich was another Sal Maglie. He would knock his mother down. He really threw hard and could intimidate a hitter. He announced in the papers about three or four days before we played the A's that he would personally stop the streak. He was going to get Joe out the first time and then walk him the next three times. Joe had to hit a bad ball off him to get

* Actually between his legs.

106

his hit. But he lined a ball right over his nose * for a single into center. The whole bench stood up and cheered Joe and laughed at Babich and called him some pretty good names.

"He got up to forty or forty-five and you really couldn't see any difference in him. He just acted the same every day. Finally the streak was over in Cleveland. Keltner made those two plays, Boudreau fielded a hard ground ball, and that was it. After the reporters left, Joe asked me to wait for him. I don't know why, I guess to keep some fans away. Lefty had pitched the game and he was gone. Now Joe gets dressed and we walk out of the gate together. He doesn't say a word. We just start walking back toward the Cleveland Hotel. We go about two blocks. I don't know what to say to comfort him so I say nothing. Finally he looks up at me with a little smile. 'Do you know if I got a hit tonight I would have made ten thousand dollars? The Heinz 57 people were following me. They wanted to make some deal with me.' Then he reached into his back pocket. 'Son of a bitch. I forgot my wallet. I left it in the park. Phil, how much money you got?' I reached into my pocket and pulled out my wallet. I had eighteen dollars. 'Let me have it.' I gave it to him and he turned toward a bar. I started in and he turned back toward me. 'No, you go on back to the hotel. I want to relax a bit.' I just left him and walked back.

"The next day he was at the ball park and never said a word about what happened the night before. He never discussed anything about it and I never brought it up. I'll tell you something else. He forgot about the money. I never asked him for it and he never returned it. That's probably the most famous eighteen dollars I ever had.

"A couple of months later we got together in Washington in the Shoreham Hotel and had a surprise party for him. Johnny Murphy handled everything and bought a beautiful silver cigarette humidor for him and we presented it to him at a special party. All the players and the press were there and he made a nice little speech."

Tommy Henrich remembered the celebration a little differently.

"I think he cried. You could see he was really touched by the whole thing. Murphy presented him with the gift and Joe accepted it and said something I'll never forget. 'I didn't know you guys felt this way about me.' Here was the greatest player in the game on this incredible streak and helping us win again and again and he didn't think we cared that much about him or the streak."

The Yankees' pitcher the night it ended was Lefty Gomez.

"Joe was probably the least excited guy in America over the streak. Guys would ask me if Joe was nervous as the streak went along and was he sleeping. You could hang him on a coat hanger in the closet and he'd fall asleep. Guys always figured he had to be nervous as the thing went on day after day. I don't know about Joe being nervous but I lost my breakfast a lot.

"Joe didn't talk much about the streak while it was on. He just went out and got a hit day after day. The night it ended in Cleveland, we jumped into a cab before the game and the driver recognized Joe and told us he had a premonition the streak would end that night. That really burned me up, especially considering how superstitious ballplayers are. People ask me if Joe had any superstitions during the streak. I don't think so. I did. I don't think I changed my underwear for two months.

"Joe hit three balls as good as you could hit balls and he didn't get a hit. Ken Keltner made two great plays at third base and Lou Boudreau handled a hot grounder at short. One of the balls to Keltner was a line drive that really exploded just back of the bag and Keltner made the play, beat Joe by a hair. What really beat Joe was the fact that he didn't get away from the plate good. Joe was usually terrific in getting away from the plate. For some reason or other, maybe because he hit the ball so hard, he got a little tangled up and was late out of the box. That cost him the hit.

"It could have been seventy-four games at least," Gomez exclaimed, referring to the fact that DiMaggio went on to hit in the next seventeen consecutive games.

Red Ruffing's recollection of Joe's emotional state was much the same.

"He didn't seem to get very excited about it. He'd come into the clubhouse every day, sit down, get a cup of coffee from Pete, read the paper for a while, get dressed, go out, and get a base hit or two. It was something to see. Everybody on the club was pulling for him."

The DiMaggio streak was one of the most extraordinary athletic feats in history. Ted Williams, who batted an astonishing .406 that year, summed it up: "I believe there isn't a record in the books that will be harder to break than Joe's fifty-six games. It may be the greatest batting achievement of all."

10: Bringing Up Scooter

The den in Phil Rizzuto's home is crowded with baseball trophies, World Series bats, a most valuable player plaque, baseball lithographs and paintings, a silver cigarette tray, and some autographed baseballs. His voice is still filled with the slang and sounds of New York.

"I was always a baseball nut. I was a little kid, about a hundred and thirty pounds, about five-foot five when I was sixteen years old, but I wanted to play. I saved the bubble gum cards and I studied all the averages. There was a sandlot team in my neighborhood run by Tony Cuccinello. He was with the Dodgers then and he would come around whenever he had an off day. He used to give us—a few of the younger kids—twenty-five dollars to fill out his team. We played in Dexter Park and played some of those good teams—the Bushwicks, the Bay Parkways, the House of David, you know those guys with the beards. One day there was a tryout in Ebbets Field for the Dodgers. Tony told me he had mentioned my name to the manager. The manager said I could come on out for a tryout. I didn't sleep all night.

"Oh, holy cow, I forgot to tell you who the manager was. It was Casey Stengel, that old son of a buck. There must have been hundreds of thousands of kids in Brooklyn who wanted to play for the Dodgers then. Well, this one day I go down to Ebbets Field. I'm sixteen years old and I am scared stiff, believe me. There must have been a hundred and fifty of us. There was some big kid, a wild right-hander —I'll never forget it—out on the mound. I get in for my first swing and he hits me right in the middle of the back with the pitch. Can you believe that? My first pitch and he hits me.

"Casey jumps up. He was watching from the dugout or some place and he comes running out. 'Go get a shoebox, kid, you're too small anyway. You can stay and watch the game.' Boy, if you think that didn't make me cry.

"The next year I went up to the Polo Grounds. The same thing. Bill Terry was the manager. He watched me run and then he sent me home. Told me I was too small. Then the

Cardinals had a tryout in Dexter Park. I went again. Same story. Now I'm really getting discouraged. But I don't want to give up. Now the Yankees schedule a tryout for Yankee Stadium. This one is going to last three days. First you run and then you field and then you hit. If they like you the first day they invite you back for the second day.

"Now it's the second day and I'm invited back in for the last day. All the Yankee coaches are there—Art Fletcher, Earle Combs, Johnny Schulte—and on the last day Joe McCarthy himself comes over. Paul Krichell was the head Yankee scout and he ran the tryout. In the middle of the third day he broke us up into teams and we played a five- or six-inning game. At the end of the day he took my name and address and told me he would contact me. In a couple of days he came over to the house and offered me a contract at seventy-five dollars a month with the Class D club at Bassett, Virginia. I later heard that the Red Sox had a scout at that tryout and he recommended they sign me. But the Boston front office turned him down because they had just signed another kid shortstop they liked named Pee Wee Reese. I went from Bassett to Norfolk to Kansas City. Now it's 1941 and I'm ordered to report to the Yankee's training camp at St. Petersburg, Florida.

"The first day was a traumatic experience. I carried this duffle bag and old Pop Logan, the clubhouse man, wouldn't let me in. He didn't think I was a ballplayer. It was embarrassing. I'm standing there trying to convince him and he refuses to budge. Now I don't know what I'm going to do. I am really scared. All of a sudden Lefty Gomez comes along. I knew him. I had played a couple of exhibition games against him at Dexter Park. He tells Logan I'm a ballplayer. 'You better let him in, Pop, before the ducks walk all over him.' Finally I'm inside the clubhouse with all these famous Yankees—DiMaggio and Dickey and Ruffing and Gordon. The only person who would talk to me was

111

Jerry Priddy. He was also a rookie and we had played to-gether at Norfolk and Kansas City. They put my locker between Dickey and Ruffing and they just talked over my head. I got dressed and went on the field. Priddy and I played catch. That was all we did for three days. The others were taking batting practice but nobody told us when to hit, so we played catch for three days.

"Finally, DiMaggio came up to me. It was the first word anybody but Priddy had spoken to me in days. 'Get in there and hit, kid.' I didn't know what to say. I just jumped into the cage behind Henrich or somebody and took five swings. I didn't do anything but hit dribblers, I was so nervous. The next round came and I hit again. This time I felt a little better and hit the ball. After that it was all right.

"Joe was the team leader but he never said much. Players just watched what he did and they tried to imitate him. If he took a bunt and five swings, they took a bunt and five swings. We'd go on these bus trips in Florida and he would sit with Lefty and Lefty would tell him funny stories and Joe would laugh and that would be it. Joe needed someone like Lefty to relieve the tension. Lefty would go all over with him. The other guys would be in the back of the bus playing cards most of the time. We barnstormed by train through Texas and Arkansas that spring and the guys would gather in Joe's berth. Everybody gravitated to him. Some-times they'd talk baseball and Joe would join in, talking about hitting or some pitchers we were going to face, and he'd be full of ideas. If the subject got off baseball he would just sit quietly and listen.

"The season started and Priddy and I made the club. We were playing pretty good and seemed to be accepted by the other guys. One day DiMaggio came up to me and asked me if I wanted to go to the movies. A new Western was playing and I agreed as fast as I could. Joe would sit so

There was nothing quiet about shy Joe DiMaggio's bat in his
debut year, as these vintage action photos demonstrate.

The young, introverted rookie in his first season with the Yankees—1936.

New York *Daily News* Photo

By October DiMaggio was already a celebrity, here showing his proud mother the sights of New York's vast harbor. His first World Series bonus would go toward a down payment on a new home for his parents.

DiMaggio at the height of his career, batting over .400 until an eye ailment caused his average to slip to .381 for the '39 season. His bachelorhood would end in November.

New York *Daily News* Photo

Vernon "Lefty" Gomez moments after pitching the Yankees to a big win in their 1937 World Series opener. Next to him, Joe D, the new home-run champ, with forty-six.

Acme Photo

Joe and Dorothy Arnold DiMaggio out on the town with Lefty Gomez and his wife, actress June O'Dea.

The Yankees' Doc Painter caring for the injury haunted outfielder.

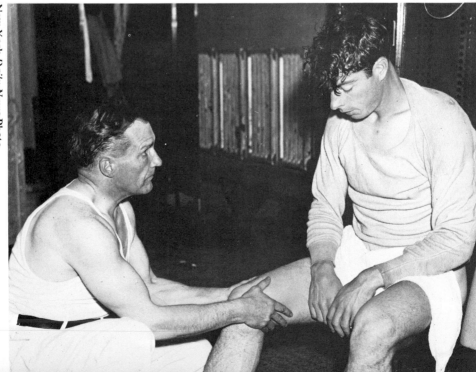

The Yankee Clipper sprints for the locker room as the fans mob him following the forty-eighth game of his incredible 1941 hitting streak.

The DiMaggios and their infant son, Joe.

Divorced after returning from military service, suffering from an ulcer, almost traded during a spate of front office maneuverings, and no longer managed by friend Joe McCarthy, DiMaggio was under great strain in 1947. Yet, as always, he maintained his stoic composure.

Joe among friends—Allie Reynolds, Gene Woodling and Jerry Coleman. New York *Daily News* Photo

Plagued by injuries and illnesses, the great star announces his retirement at the Yankees' New York office, sharing the inevitable moment with George Weiss, Casey Stengel and club owners Del Webb and Dan Topping. New York *Daily News* Photo

Moments later, Joe fights back tears. Above him is a mural showing the young DiMaggio in his prime.

DiMaggio and the admirers he always felt comfortable with.

Retirement came easily, with lots of time for his new found golfing passion, and a romance that culminated in elopement and marriage to a budding film star—Marilyn Monroe.

Joe and his bride honeymooning in Japan, and dining out at the chic Stork Club. Two hundred and seventy-four days after their nuptial, Norma Jeane Di-Maggio (Marilyn Monroe) filed for divorce.

The great stars of yesterday at a 1971 reunion. Left to right: Phil Rizzuto, Bobby Brown, Don Larsen, Allie Reynolds, Yogi Berra, Billy Martin, Whitey Ford, Mickey Mantle and—the man they save for last—Joe D.

Nineteen-year-old Joseph Paul DiMaggio of the San Francisco Seals.

still in the movie you would think he was asleep. He just liked to relax in a movie. He was really an introvert, had this bad ulcer, and the movie was some place he could feel completely at ease.

"The season ended, we won the pennant, and now we are playing the Dodgers in the World Series. You can imagine how nervous I am. Holy cow. Anyway, Gomez comes up to me before the first game and asks me if I'm nervous. I tell him I sure am. He tells me, 'Listen, kid, when I get in there and I get in trouble I'll call time. Your mother and all your friends from Brooklyn are at the game, right? You just come on over from shortstop. Can you imagine your mother telling all those people how the great Lefty Gomez is asking my son what to do?' That made me laugh and really calmed me down.

"The game I remember best, I guess everybody does, was the fourth game. That's the one where Henrich swung and missed and the catcher, Mickey Owen, missed the ball. The Dodgers were ahead 4–3 in the top of the ninth. I was sitting there on the bench and it was two out and bases empty. Henrich is up. I'm sitting in the corner of the dugout and I'm holding all the gloves in my lap. I didn't want any of them to get lost in the excitement of the game. Henrich swings and misses for strike three. I turn toward the runway with the gloves. Then I hear the crowd screaming. All hell breaks loose. Henrich is safe. DiMaggio gets a hit, Keller hits a double off the wall, Dickey walks, and Gordon hits a wall. We get four runs and it's over the next day. After the Series I get a call from Joe. This was probably the most important call of my life. I was home in Brooklyn with my mother and we were still talking about the Series. Joe tells me his wife, Dorothy, had just given birth to a son, Joe Junior, and that it had been a breech birth and that the boy was born with these two huge strawberries on his face.

113

Joe said he had to get over to the hospital to see his wife and the boy. I congratulated him but I couldn't quite figure out why he had gone into all this detail.

"Then he tells me he was scheduled to do a banquet that night for his friend Jimmy Ceres in New Jersey. Jimmy Ceres used to take Joe to all these fancy Italian restaurants. Jimmy used to go with a girl whose father was a fire chief in Newark. The fire chief had asked Jimmy to get Joe DiMaggio for this big banquet they had planned, a benefit for the fire department. Now Joe can't go and he asks me to substitute. I figured the people would be mad as hell. Here they were expecting Joe DiMaggio and they get a rookie. I agreed to go for Joe. The people were nice. Probably because I was Italian like Joe they accepted me. I talked for a few minutes about the Series, signed a few autographs, and that was it.

"Now the fire chief, Emil Esselborn, asks me to come back to his house for a cup of coffee. I'm sitting there drinking coffee and all of a sudden his daughter Cora comes down the stairs. Holy cow. You know ballplayers. I went crazy. I asked her for a date right away. I didn't go home for three months. I took a room at the Douglas Hotel. I took her out every night. Cora was working as a model and I would pick her up at work every day, go to a movie, go to dinner, go dancing.

"I took her to dinner at this real nice restaurant. The snow is coming down and it's a beautiful scene. We are sitting at a window seat and I propose to her. She says no. I got so goddamn mad. I couldn't believe it. Here I was, a Yankee baseball player. I had a good future, I had just played in the World Series, and she turned me down. I got in my car and I drove to Norfolk, where I had played, and stayed there to sulk. Then I get a call from my mother. It was December 7, 1941. I had heard the news on the radio. Now my mother calls and says that Lefty had just called and told her the Japs were right outside Brooklyn and I'd better get right home.

"I came home, saw Cora again, and proposed again. She turned me down again. I didn't know it but she was studying to become a Catholic. That's why she was turning me down. She wanted to finish instructions before she would marry me.

"We won the pennant again in 1942 and the Cardinals beat us in the World Series. I knew I was about to be drafted so I enlisted in the Navy. Some captain had called me from Norfolk and told me I could play ball if I enlisted on a certain date. The last day of the World Series was October 5. I had to report to Norfolk on October 6.

"After the final game Joe and Dorothy invited Cora and me over to their apartment. It was a penthouse in Manhattan. Joe Junior was in a crib in another room. Dorothy cooked dinner and we stayed up all night talking and drinking. It was my farewell party before joining the Navy. Cora and Dorothy got along real good, but Joe would get a little moody and leave for a few minutes every so often. He didn't like the idea of sitting and talking all night with the women. Dorothy was lovely, a beautiful woman, very solid person. I guess Joe was tough to live with. His whole world was baseball. When you marry a beautiful woman she wants to be seen. I think Joe never really understood that."

Joe enlisted a short time later.

11: The Yankee Wars

The big boys were back in 1946 as the Yankees gathered for spring training in Panama. Joe DiMaggio had been away for three years, returning as an Army Air Force sergeant. He had spent most of his enlistment playing baseball for the troops, running clinics, dining with generals, and showing baseball films. During that time he had developed an ulcer and been divorced by his wife. "There were times," she had tearfully told the judge, "when he wouldn't talk to me for weeks." Their son, Joe Junior, was four.

"Dorothy was a lovely lady," Toots Shor recalled. "She really loved Joe. I don't know why it broke up. I guess because Joe wouldn't pay her enough attention. Joe liked to be with George Solotaire or in my joint or with Cannon and some of the other sportswriters. I don't think Dorothy liked that part of it. Then if Joe would have two oh-for-four days in a row and the Yankees would lose both of them, look out. He was really tough to handle. He would really sulk. Like I say, he felt the whole team depended on him. He never showed it, but Joe worried a lot."

The Yankees hadn't won a pennant in the last two seasons that Joe and the other veterans had been away. Everyone thought the Yankees could recapture their rightful place on top now that DiMaggio, Henrich, Keller, and the rest were back from service.

All of them had a tougher time getting in shape than they had expected. DiMaggio started the season poorly and never really found his stride. He batted under .300 for the first time in his career, failed to knock in his usual minimum of 100 runs, had only 25 home runs, suffered various new injuries, and watched his brother Dom's team, the Boston Red Sox, win the pennant. For thirty-one-year-old DiMaggio, it was his worst year in the major leagues. A great season for anyone else, for him it was a disaster.

The bad season was made somewhat bearable by the presence on the team of a cherubic young pitcher named Joe Page. He had begun following DiMaggio around in spring training, and Joe, who always seemed to need a shield from the public and the press, accepted the lively Irishman as the perfect pal. But where Lefty Gomez had been the quiet young DiMaggio's mentor, Page was his disciple. He would dress like Joe, imitate him, and do his bidding under the guise of friendship. Teammates started referring to him as "DiMaggio's porter" but the young pitcher didn't seem to care.

"Page just liked being around DiMaggio," pitcher Eddie Lopat later recalled. "It made him feel good and it made him feel important. DiMaggio needed a guy like that, a guy he could call on to be his company when he wanted somebody. I think DiMaggio was the loneliest man I ever knew. He couldn't even eat a meal in a hotel restaurant. The fans just wouldn't let him. He led the league in room service.

"Page would always be there if DiMaggio wanted company. DiMaggio would come into the clubhouse and ask for a cup of coffee. Page would yell, 'Me too, Pete,' to the clubhouse guy. We all started calling Page 'Me too.' He didn't mind. Nothing ever bothered Page."

"I don't care," Page would say, pointing to DiMaggio. "That's Big Joe over there; he's my pal."

Besides Page, DiMaggio also spent a lot of time with ticket broker George Solotaire, whom he lived with for a while in an apartment off Broadway. Using his extensive show business connections, Solotaire would constantly provide DiMaggio with beautiful showgirls to date. Given Joe's fame, it wasn't difficult, so DiMaggio would often be seen escorting a budding starlet to the Copa, El Morocco, Latin Quarter, or Harwyn Club. But there were no serious involvements.

The Yankee front office was also going through a trying period just after the war. Colonel Jacob Ruppert, the owner, and general manager Ed Barrow were gone. The team now belonged to Dan Topping, a millionaire sportsman, and to industrialist Del Webb.

Larry MacPhail was the man the two partners brought

in to run the club as general manager. He was—and is —bombastic, flamboyant, and outspoken. During World War I he was involved in a wild attempt to abduct the Kaiser, and although the plan to bag the monarch failed, MacPhail managed to capture the Kaiser's ashtray. It still sits on his desk, like a trophy, in recognition of his stormy eighty-four years on this earth.

"I guess the worst time I ever had with the Yankees was with Joe McCarthy. His last season was 1946 and he was in bad shape. He was drinking too much and he wasn't eating right and he was worried about the team because it was playing so lousy."

Unable to get along with MacPhail, Joe McCarthy left the team on May 24. Joe DiMaggio seemed deeply hurt by his old friend's departure. Catcher Bill Dickey, finishing his last season, took his place.

"Dickey really didn't want the job. Then he takes it and in September, after we know we are not going to win, he comes to me and asks for a contract for 1947."

MacPhail refused to grant a contract for the next season until the current year was past. Dickey quit.

"He left my office and I made Johnny Neun the manager, but I never really considered him permanent. I wanted a man with experience. The Yankees were changing. Those *old* players were being phased out and I needed an experienced guy."

The maneuverings and politics created a lot of turmoil, especially for rookies like Vic Raschi. Raschi threw bullets for the Yankees that year—the first of many years—his face stern as he peered intently at a hitter before firing the ball.

"No rookie ever broke in to a more confused situation than me. I arrived at Yankee Stadium in September 1946 and as soon as I got there they told me I would be starting the game. There I was a rookie, my first day with the Yankees, and I was on the mound. There were two other rookies in the lineup—we had been called up from Newark together—Yogi Berra and Bobby Brown.

"I think I was still in my street clothes trying to get adjusted to the big clubhouse when I heard some of the other players talking. They leaned over and told me the story. Bill Dickey had gone up to the office and been fired and coach Johnny Neun was the manager. I don't know who made up the lineup card but I was on it.

"I would only talk to the other rookies, Berra and Brown. I could see DiMaggio dressing over on the other side of the room but I wouldn't dare go over and introduce myself. It just wasn't done. Not even in the minor leagues. The stars came over to you when they were ready. You just kept your mouth shut and did your job. The Yankees were always like that. A rookie that talked too much would be in trouble. First they wanted to see if you could play.

"I got out of that clubhouse, walked up that runway, and went into the dugout. I took one look at the field and I could hardly believe it. It was huge, so large. It could make you nervous just looking at it, before you even tried to throw a ball to an opposition hitter."

The machinations in the Yankee management resulted in some strange and secret negotiations. The biggest was about Joe. Ted Williams and Joe DiMaggio were simply the best players in baseball and constant rivals for press attention, league records, and annual honors. Though the two were inevitably pitted against each other, the great Boston slugger had often been overshadowed by the mighty DiMaggio, partly because of the power and prestige of the New York press and partly because of Williams' open antagonism toward reporters and fans. Given DiMaggio's greater fielding, running, and throwing abilities, it was understandable that many would play down the volatile Williams while lauding the gentlemanly DiMaggio.

In late April 1947 Boston owner Tom Yawkey and Yankee owner Dan Topping met at Toots Shor's and talked late into the night. The deal they were discussing was the trade of Ted Williams for Joe DiMaggio.* Though Ted Williams was the darling of the Boston owner, who treated him like a lovable but incorrigible son, business was business. Besides, it could truly benefit the two players. The idiosyncracies of their home fields were not suited to their hitting strengths. If the deal went through, left-handed Williams would have Yankee Stadium's short right-field wall to go for, and right-handed DiMaggio could aim for Fenway Park's short left-field wall. It could allow the two great hitters many more home runs than they were getting now—perhaps even a shot at Ruth's record.

After many hours Topping and Yawkey tentatively agreed—Williams for DiMaggio. Yawkey would sleep on it and call Topping in the morning. The call came promptly the next day.

"What about it?" Topping asked. "Do we have a deal?"

"Well, I want to make it, but I just can't make it even up. The people in Boston think Williams is better."

Ted Williams was batting well and had been named the most valuable player the previous year, while Joe had not come back as strong as expected. Also, DiMaggio was four years older. The rationale was questionable but a handy negotiating point.

Yawkey suggested a compromise. "I'll tell you what. It's a deal if you throw in your little left fielder."

Topping knew it was the end. He could explain—possibly—trading one great star for another. But he could not and would not dare to try rationalizing anything else. The

* Substantiated by Del Webb, Toots Shor and Larry MacPhail.

two owners agreed—the deal was off. No more would be said about it. Williams would remain in Boston; Joe would stay in New York, along with "the little left fielder," a rookie named Yogi Berra.

"Joe wasn't my hero when I came to the Yankees, even though he was Italian. I grew up in St. Louis and Joe Medwick was my idol. I idolized DiMag after I played with him —because he could play so good. I was happy to be on the same team with him. I used to watch him around the clubhouse and I would do whatever he did. That's how I learned to act. On the field he was just a perfect player. I was a left-handed hitter and he was right-handed, so I didn't learn that much, but we used to talk about hitting and what a guy would throw you in a certain spot. He wasn't afraid to give you advice if you asked him for it. But he wouldn't rush up to you like some guys do and start telling you you're doing this wrong and you're doing that wrong.

"Joe was the star of the team, so nobody ever really bothered him much. He went by himself most of the time, but once in a while he would ask me out to dinner. He always paid. He wouldn't let you pick up a check, so after you were out with him a couple of times, you knew he was going to pay so you didn't even offer. The check came, you said, 'Thanks, Joe,' and that was it. He just said, 'I invited you so I pay.' You couldn't argue with him."

Bobby Brown, Yogi's roommate, was the other rookie taken aboard that year. Intent on becoming a doctor, third baseman Brown played baseball only as a sideline. He is now a cardiologist in Fort Worth, Texas.

"Joe was simply the greatest all-around ballplayer I ever saw. That was the height of his popularity then. There were so many people after him, night and day, that the ball park seemed like the only place he could really rest. There was enormous pressure on him, on and off the field.

"Joe didn't show much emotion. He was ready when he got on the field and he just played, and played better than anybody else could."

In 1947 the Yankees got a new manager, Bucky Harris, who was hired over his own objections by Larry MacPhail after Dickey and Neun were released. It also appeared likely that the Yankees would soon have one less pitcher. Joe Page had kept saving himself the previous season with good performances at crucial moments but now seemed destined for the minors. DiMaggio, his roommate, kept on encouraging him, suggesting ways of improving his control and advising him on how to pitch to certain hitters.

"Why don't you quit worrying?" DiMaggio told him one night as Page tossed and turned in bed while Joe tried to sleep. "The game is a lot easier if you don't worry about it off the field." *That* from the player who probably brooded more than anyone about his performance!

On May 10 the Yankees played in Boston. Page pitched poorly and wanted to talk about it with Joe over dinner after the game. But DiMaggio was dining with some friends and was unavailable. Alone, Page went on a binge and returned to their hotel well after midnight. DiMaggio, already in bed, was roused by Page's noisy drunken entrance.

"He gave me hell," Page recalled. "He said I was letting myself down and letting the team down. I was ruining my own chances."

The dressing-down sobered the young pitcher, who vowed to be more careful and think through his ambitions and conduct. The next morning DiMaggio went to Red Patterson, then the traveling secretary of the team, and said that he had decided he wanted a room by himself and would pay the difference. Patterson naturally obliged. That was the only reason DiMaggio ever gave Patterson or anyone else.

"I was grateful about that," Page later confessed.

Although DiMaggio stopped sharing quarters with Page, he did not sever the friendship. They still dined and traveled together, relaxed at Toots Shor's, and went to the movies, Page buying the tickets while DiMaggio waited in a cab so as not to be recognized. Yet despite the lecture and the separation, Page remained shaky. By May 26 he was very close to being shipped out. That Monday night the Yankees were trailing the Red Sox 3–1 before a sellout crowd in Yankee Stadium. Two men were on base and nobody was out. With nearly seventy-five thousand people watching, Joe Page was called into the game. As always, he jumped over the low bullpen fence in right field and sauntered toward the mound. The ultimate test had come.

The first batter was none other than Ted Williams. The count went to three balls and no strikes. A walk would knock Page out of the game and down to the minors. One pitch from oblivion, Joe Page threw a strike. And then another. The next pitch was a good strike too, but Williams hit it weakly toward first base. The ball somehow twisted off the first baseman's glove and suddenly the bases were loaded.

Manager Bucky Harris fumed on the bench. Page walked around the mound and glanced at center field, where Di-Maggio was plucking at the grass.

Rudy York was up. Again the count went to three balls and no strikes. The fourth pitch—miraculously—was a strike, followed by another, then a high fast ball. York swung mightily, and missed. The crowd exploded. One out, bases loaded.

The dangerous Bobby Doerr came up to bat. Incredibly Page fell behind again—three balls, no strikes. You could imagine the Yankee manager's hair turning gray. Page threw two fast strikes, followed by a wicked fast ball. Doerr swung and missed for strike three. Two down.

The next man up swung at the first pitch and hit a soft

123

flyball into right field. Tommy Henrich caught it easily and the Yankees were out of the inning without a run scored against them. The Bronx Bombers had squeaked by. Joe DiMaggio stepped into the batter's box in the next inning and hit a home run. Then the famous Yankee momentum took over. Page was perfect the rest of the way and the Yanks won 9–3.

Joe Page was suddenly a hero and went on that year to establish himself as the best relief pitcher in the league. In fact, the Yankees won the pennant and Page starred in the World Series against the Dodgers.

"Joe Page was a real likable guy," according to Eddie Lopat. "He was always smiling, always friendly, and always giving his best. You would look at him sometimes in the clubhouse and know that he had had a long night. He would sort of walk out to that bullpen before the game in a sleepy trance. Then the game would start and he would come alive. Once he got that call and leaped over the bullpen fence he was a new man, really full of fight, a hell of a competitor and a guy who gave everything he had. I never really could figure out the relationship between Joe Page and Joe Di-Maggio, but I guess when you are as famous as Joe DiMaggio you need a Joe Page. I'm glad I never got that famous."

By the end of the long season the strain had become terrific for DiMaggio. His divorce, his friend Joe McCarthy's firing, the management politics, the insistent fans, his role on the team, his own internal drive to play all-out all the time—these took their toll. But the tension showed itself only rarely.

"In all the years I played with Joe, I think I only saw him get mad once," Phil Rizzuto recalled. "That was in the World Series of '47 when he hit that long fly ball in the sixth game with two on and Al Gionfriddo caught it in front of the bullpen. Joe was at second base when Gionfriddo caught it and Joe smacked the base loose from its hinges and kicked some dirt free. He was really steamed. You couldn't blame him." Brooklyn won 8–6.

Still, it was otherwise a fine year, and Joe DiMaggio was again elected the most valuable player.

12: Pain

Baseball reached its peak of postwar prosperity in the summer of 1948. The Cleveland Indians, under the guidance of promotional genius Bill Veeck, won the pennant in a one-game playoff with the Boston Red Sox and drew more than 2,600,000 people. The Yankees, in Bucky Harris' final year as manager, finished third and yet drew nearly 2,400,-000 people to Yankee Stadium—just a little less than the champs.

Joe DiMaggio had another marvelous year in 1948, at age thirty-three. It was his last really big season. He batted .320, led the league with 155 runs batted in and 39 home runs, and scored 110 runs. That record won him his first hundred-thousand-dollar contract, for the 1949 season.

But DiMaggio had reached advanced middle age, as ballplayers count their summers. When a baseball player moves past thirty, his body begins to betray him. It does not escape injury as easily as it once did, and it does not rebound from injury as swiftly. The player may look and feel the same. He may fool himself with a good spring or a fine season, but there is a steady loss of physical skills. Some, like Willie Mays, Hank Aaron, Ted Williams, and Stan Musial, delay the inevitable until well past forty. Others, still young men, are torn apart by injury and illness.

DiMaggio had always played hard. Every muscle in his body at one time or another had suffered from the pulling, ripping, and tearing of his more than twenty years as an athlete. The final assault came in midsummer of 1948, when his right heel began aching. From that point on, DiMaggio never again played baseball without pain.

From spring training of 1948 through the 1951 season, DiMaggio became the main concern of the team's new physician, Dr. Sidney Gaynor. Gaynor did not perform the surgery on DiMaggio's heel, but it fell upon him to care for it and for the endless series of ailments that would plague Joe for the next four years. Doc Gaynor is still team physician of the New York Yankees.

"It was the spring of 1948. I had driven down to Florida from New York and after I arrived I went over to the clubhouse at Huggins Field in St. Petersburg to meet trainer Gus Mauch and talk with him.

"The workout was over when I got there. I walked through the clubhouse and it was empty. There were only two people in the room—Joe DiMaggio and Pete Sheehy, the clubhouse man. DiMaggio was naked. He was standing in front of a long mirror and he seemed to be mumbling to himself. He was checking his backside and seemed to be examining a red mark, a bruise on his bottom. He looked at the mirror and at his backside for a couple of minutes. Sheehy was going about his business. The bruise was in a difficult spot to catch in the mirror. He turned to Sheehy and called him over. 'Hey, Pete, take a look at this. Is there a bruise there?'

"Sheehy never changed his expression. He walked by and said, 'Sure there is, Joe. It's from all those guys kissing your ass.'

"DiMaggio didn't have any serious problems that spring. His heel began to bother him in the early part of the regular season. It was very bad by midsummer but he kept playing on it. DiMaggio ran flat-footed. It's probably why he had problems with both heels. He was putting an extreme amount of pressure on the heels and had done it for very many years.

"We tried everything to relieve the pressure on the heel but nothing helped. As the season went on it really ached. Surgery would be the only answer. The Yankees decided to take DiMaggio to a doctor who specialized in that kind of surgery. Joe was examined by several different guys. They all recommended immediate surgery but the Yankees and DiMaggio wanted to wait until the season was over. Joe had a big year and now they decided to do the work.

"Larry MacPhail was a guy who knew everybody. He had this doctor friend who had done some work on several of the players. Now they sent DiMaggio to him. The guy apparently had a big reputation but this time he was out of his field. The guy was a general surgeon but this called for somebody with specific experience and training in this field. For some reason or other, I don't know why, DiMaggio and the Yankees decided to let this doctor do the job. Well, he really screwed it up. A spur is a growth of bone at the intersection of the tendon. It is really an arthritic manifestation. In DiMaggio's case it was probably caused by years of shock and trauma to the heel area from the constant pounding it took on so many outfields over the years. The spur had probably been there at the heel for many, many years, but an inflammation was developing that was causing great pain.

"Finally this guy did the operation. He did it all wrong. He used a horrible incision and went into the heel at the wrong point. He went around the heel instead of going through it. He peeled everything back and attacked the spur from the opposite end. He affected the circulation very badly. It just never healed properly. A complication developed called osteitis. Joe couldn't walk on it for a long time. Then when the cast was removed and examined it just wasn't healing properly. The following April they took him to Johns Hopkins and Dr. George Bennett operated on

127

him again to repair the damage the first doctor had inflicted. Dr. Bennett was very prominent in that field. After that operation it simply became a question of healing by itself.

"Dr. Bennett did a real good job of repairing the heel. He had to perform plastic surgery on the area and actually rebuild it and repair the circulation. It was a hell of an operation. It was amazing that DiMaggio was back in the lineup as fast as he was.

"Joe played hurt almost all the time. He had a high tolerance for pain and could play when other people wouldn't. That's just something built into the man. Besides the heel, his major problems were a bad knee, bad shoulder, and bad elbow. His shoulder was chronically lame. All the things were caused by wear and tear. The tendons become arthritic after so many years of punishing them. There is simply no way to prevent those kinds of things from happening to a ballplayer who plays as hard and as long as Joe did. The body simply can't fight off all those stresses and strains.

"Joe didn't complain about the injuries. He wasn't a bellyacher. If he was hurt he would tell you, and you would do what you could and that was it. He didn't want sympathy. He just wanted to be able to play.

"I remember one time we were coming across that ferry they used to have in Sarasota to St. Petersburg before they built that fancy bridge. I was on the ferry with the team after a spring-training game and DiMaggio came up to me. He put out his arm and touched his right shoulder. 'Hey, Doc, feel this.' I put my hand on his shoulder and touched it a little. He winced with some pain. I told him he had some thickness in the shoulder but nothing serious. He asked me what I could do about it.

" 'There isn't much you can do about something like that. If the thickness gets worse, we'll operate on the

128

shoulder and take it out.' This was late in his career and I didn't think he wanted to undergo any more surgery.

"'If it doesn't work out, I can always do pick-and-shovel work. Right, Doc?'

"I spent a lot of time with DiMaggio on the field, in the clubhouse, in the training room, and in hospitals. He never talked about himself or his private life. He didn't discuss personal matters. He just discussed yesterday's game or today's game or tomorrow's pitcher or something like that.

"He was always a coffee hound and a heavy smoker. Now he drinks tea and has given up cigarettes. In those days nobody knew about things like that. He took good care of himself and he worked hard. In his last year or two minor injuries bothered him a lot—a muscle pull or a severe bruise, something like that—things that he would have shaken off when he was younger. He didn't recover from his aches and pains as rapidly. That probably made him quit as much as anything.

"I remember the last couple of games of the '49 season against the Red Sox. That was the year he started late because of the heel injury. Then he came back and played until September. He had a viral pneumonia and was out from the middle of September. It was one of those things that started as a cold and just grew worse. He was tired and run down and couldn't fight it off. He was in the hopsital for a few days and out of the lineup for about three weeks. Then he came back to play the last two games of the season. He looked very bad. He was weak and haggard. But he had a big series and the Yankees won the pennant.

"DiMaggio wasn't a guy you could kid around with in the training room. He was a very serious person. I see him now and I am amazed how he greets people and laughs and gets along with everybody. I guess that's what happens when you stay away from the game for a while. I guess

129

everybody changes. Look at me giving you all this inside information. I used to be a crusty old bastard."

Eddie Lopat, the Yankee left-hander, was famous for his three pitching speeds—slow, slower, and slowest. Lopat was a master of the off-speed pitch, a master of deception. Stylish and smooth on the mound, he put his pitching knowledge and skills to good advantage, using off-speed and weird pitches—like screw balls, changes, and palm balls —to win regularly. He was a very tenacious competitor.

"DiMaggio? He was a perfectionist. I remember pitching against him for a couple of years when I was with the White Sox. I used to get him out with the screw ball. That was always a tough pitch for any right-hander to hit. Then he just studied me and the pitch and he mastered it after a while. He hurt me a few times when he got base hits off the screw ball. There was no way to pitch him and get away with it regularly. He was too smart a hitter for that.

"He just knew the ins and outs like nobody else. This one time after I joined the Yankees, we were playing a tough game against Cleveland. Lou Boudreau, who was always a tough hitter for me, was up. There were a couple of guys on, and I turned around to rub up the ball and check the outfield. DiMaggio was playing straight away on Boudreau. That was the way I expected it. But I throw two pitches and I'm off the plate and I'm behind two and nothing. The next pitch has to be a strike. I throw a fast ball over the middle of the plate and Boudreau socks it. It was a line drive over Rizzuto's head at shortstop and I figured it would go through the gap for a double or a triple and I would be gone. All of a sudden I turn and look up. The ball is hanging up and DiMaggio is catching it in left center field. I couldn't believe it. When the inning was over I asked him about the play. 'When you went to two and oh,' he said 'I moved about seventy or eighty feet into left center. I knew you wouldn't let him pull the ball when you started working on him so I played straight away. When the count went to two and oh I figured you had to come in with a pitch so that's when I moved.'

"I never talked much to Joe around the clubhouse. My locker was near his but he wasn't one for small talk. Joe was hurting a lot when I was there. He used to come in after a game, have a beer, take off his shoes, and just sit in front of his locker. He always gave so much of himself on the field that there wasn't much left when the game was over. I think his legs and feet really bothered him a lot when he got older. That happens to a lot of players. You could almost see Joe breathe easier when he could come into the clubhouse after a game and get those shoes off."

Like Doc Gaynor, Lopat remembers well the last two dramatic games in 1949.

"Birdie Tebbetts was with the Red Sox then and he was a pretty good needler. The Red Sox had just signed a kid for a fifty-thousand-dollar bonus and Tebbetts was telling a couple of us about it before the game. Then he says, 'I'm not jealous. We'll win the pennant and I'll make almost as much as that kid this year with my World Series money.' Then the game starts and the Red Sox get ahead 4–0. You could hear Tebbetts' voice all over the park. He's really ripping into us and bragging about how much money he was going to make and all that. Now we start to catch them, get a couple of runs, get a couple more, and finally win the game. Tebbetts was the last batter for the Red Sox and hit a high popup to first base. Henrich was over there and he caught it and the game was over. As Tebbetts ran by, everybody let him have it. 'Go borrow some money from the kid.' Things like that. DiMaggio stopped all that nonsense. He said 'Let's win tomorrow.' We had forgotten we still had to beat them one more time before we really could talk. Joe didn't forget. He never forgot anything.

"Joe hurt a lot in 1949 but it was a great season for him. He really hit great after he came back. It was a big season for me too. I had never been on a pennant winner so I was real excited going down the stretch. There was a lot of pride involved. When you were with the Yankees, then you knew you were the best."

Vic Raschi: "Everybody who was on the club remembers how Joe came back in '49 from the heel thing and then when he was sick at the end of the year. The night before the Red Sox weekend series, I went out to dinner with Reynolds and Lopat. We went to Mama Leone's and we walked in there and saw half a dozen Red Sox players and they were having a good time. We talked with them a little bit. They wished us luck and we wished them luck, but you know that none of us really meant it.

"The next day we came into the clubhouse the same time as always. It was so quiet and calm you could hear a pin drop. That was different because there used to be a lot of cutting up. I could feel the sweat in the palm of my hands.

"We all knew what we had to do that day. Joe had been sick and nobody expected him to make the lineup. All of a sudden he's in there. It was a big lift for everybody. He led by his excellence on the field, and just having him out there, as sick as he was, had to be important to all of us. He was weak but he knew all the hitters in the league so well that if you made a mistake you figured he would run it down and save you anyway. We beat them that day and we beat them the next day and Joe got a couple of big hits and we won the pennant. He didn't get too excited after the game. He had won so many by then that I guess he just expected to win and nothing was surprising about it.

"He was tense in those days. The pressure was always enormous, always on him, and he felt like he just had to carry the club. He never seemed able to let down and just

132

enjoy himself. I was with him more than five years and I saw him do some impossible things. He was the best there was. Make no mistake about that. You ask all the ballplayers who played with him in those days. I'll bet you they will tell you the same thing."

Allie Reynolds was nicknamed Superchief for his explosive fast ball and his part-Indian background. He relished the tough games.

"I thanked Joe many times for engineering my trade to the Yankees. I always told him I was glad I didn't make him look bad. I was happy when they made the deal. I knew the Yankees were a lot more stable team than Cleveland and I had a chance to win a lot more baseball games. That's just about how it worked out.

"I had a couple of good years with Cleveland but my wildness had kept me from winning more games. I seemed to cure that with regular work with the Yankees. The Yankees were such a good club that they kept you in a lot of games when you didn't have your stuff by scoring a lot of runs. That was the big thing about the Yankees in those days. They could beat you in a lot of ways. If they needed defense they got defense. If they needed more hitting that's what they got.

"When I was with the Indians and faced Joe, he gave me a lot of trouble. Nobody was very successful against Joe. He was just a great hitter. Being a right-hander helped me a little against him because my fast ball tailed away, but he could still go out and get it. He was pretty quick with that bat.

"I came to the Yankees in the spring of '47 and things were a little strange for me. I was thirty-two years old then and a lot of the writers thought I was finished. I had a terrible spring and my elbow was bothering me all the time. They sent me to Johns Hopkins and they told me rest and warm weather would cure it. I had heard that before and I wasn't really that sure. I was worried about my career and I thought I might be finished. The big thing about baseball, especially pitching, is you never know when it will be all over. You can go at any minute. Then the warm weather came in early May and I was all right."

Reynolds won nineteen games and lost only eight for the Yankees in 1947, won a game in the World Series against the Dodgers, and firmly established himself as the ace of the Yankee staff.

"The next season I was fine. I had a locker on the other side of the room so we never really talked much, Joe and I. Lopat was near him and I think he kidded Joe a lot, but that was about it. There was a lot of horseplay when we won but Joe was never part of that. He didn't remain aloof. It just didn't seem right to give Joe DiMaggio a hotfoot or snap a wet towel at him like guys did at most of the other guys. If there was a serious discussion about the game or about any of the other players, Joe would get into that and give his opinion, and most of the time his opinion really helped win ball games. He knew an awful lot about every pitcher and every hitter in the league. He really studied the game.

"One thing about Joe that nobody really understands. I don't think they knew it then either. He gave a thousand percent every game, day in and day out, for a lot of years. That takes a great deal out of a man. Baseball is a tough game, physically and mentally. People don't understand how it wears a man down, the pressure and the aches and the summer heat. It's a real tough life and I think it's a lot tougher for a great player like Joe DiMaggio. He had to do it every single day. People came to see him play and do well. They paid good money and they expected a spectacular performance out of him every day. That's impossible. But a guy who has laid down a five-dollar bill doesn't want to hear about your aches and pains. He just wants a great performance. If Joe didn't hit a home run or make a great catch, people went home disappointed.

"Joe was going through a lot of pain at the end. Stengel moved him to first base once and Joe didn't like it. He felt uncomfortable. I think Casey wanted Joe to move to right field. He thought it would be easier on him. Joe didn't want to do that. He felt if he couldn't play center field, he couldn't play. I think if he had moved to right field a couple of years earlier he might have played another year or two. I really believe that. I think shortstop and center field really take a lot out of a man when he is older. There's a lot of running to do. You don't see too many forty-year-olds playing short-stop or center field. Sometimes you see some older pitchers who can get by on finesse.

"I remember how it happened with me. I was having back trouble and I couldn't pop the ball like I wanted to. Some hitters were getting hits off me who shouldn't have been touching me. I couldn't strike out a guy when I wanted. Joe was the same way. He couldn't pull a pitch and hit a live fast ball at the end when he wanted to. He used to be able to do that just about any time he got a good ball, when I first joined the club.

"My back started bothering me real bad in '53 and got worse in '54. I hardly could ever pitch without some pain. I didn't have any stamina. I just would go out there and throw and guys would hit me. I used to be the kind of guy who couldn't wait to pitch. The days in between used to drive me crazy. I wanted that ball, I wanted to go after those hitters. Then my back started acting up and that's all I thought about. I would sit around for a couple of days and then it would be my turn and I would think, 'Gosh, I have to pitch again,' That's no way to play baseball.

"I had a pretty good year in '54 and they wanted me to come back for the next season, but I didn't want to do it any more. I knew I couldn't help the club or myself. If I went back, I would just be fooling myself and everybody else. I would be out there spinning my wheels instead of really making some contribution to the ball club.

"Joe used to be a very intense man. He isn't that way any more at all. The pressure is off him now. If he was like this then, he probably wouldn't have been as great a player as he was. Joe was very serious about baseball. You don't get to be the best player in the game without working very hard at it and without being very serious. I learned a lot about baseball just watching Joe DiMaggio take the field."

13: Trouble with Stengel

The Yankees finished a disappointing third in the 1948 season. With Bucky Harris fired, it had fallen upon the new general manager George Weiss to restore the Yankees to their accustomed place at the top. Casey Stengel was the new manager he chose for the task. Stengel was managing in the minor leagues, at Oakland. At fifty-eight, he was considered finished. Actually, he had hardly begun.

Phil Rizzuto spoke candidly about the trouble between Stengel and DiMaggio.

"Baseball wasn't much fun for Joe from 1949 until he quit. He was getting older and he was hurt a lot. The worst thing of all, Casey Stengel was the manager. Casey came to the club in '49 from the Coast League and the first thing he tells us is that we are a veteran club, we know how to play, he doesn't know the American League, and he will let us run the club ourselves. We hardly had any signs that first year. Guys knew when to bunt, when to hit and run, all by themselves. Casey was a great manager in '49. He hardly managed. Now comes '50. It was my best year on the field. It was my most aggravating year with Stengel.

"Casey began clowning around more, playing up to the writers, juggling the lineup, and saying things behind guys' backs. One day he made some crazy move—left-handed hitter for a right-handed hitter late in a game we were winning by eight runs or something—and Joe says to me, 'This guy doesn't have to make all these moves to win. He's got the writers buffaloed.'

"You should have seen the way he picked a pinch hitter. He would walk up and down the bench stopping at every guy and saying, 'You don't look like you can hit this pitcher.' Then he would stop in front of one guy and say, 'Get a bat.' One time we were playing the White Sox and Chico Carrasquel was playing pretty good shortstop for them. Casey picked up a bat and walked up and down the dugout looking for a pinch hitter. Then he picks the guy. I forget who it was. 'Don't hit a grounder to that shortstop.' He sends the guy to the plate and, sure enough, the guy hits a grounder to Carrasquel for a double play. 'I told him not to hit there! I told him not to hit there!' Casey was really screaming. The poor guy had to hide in the corner of the dugout for the next week.

"Another thing about Casey made me mad. He would sit on the bench and rip the guys in the game. 'This guy can't make the play.' 'This guy couldn't hit this pitcher with a pole.' Things like that. We figured he was ripping us too when we weren't there. Maybe he wanted that stuff to get back to the player. Maybe he thought it would make the guy play harder to show him up. I don't know. But it made me uncomfortable.

"I think the real trouble with DiMaggio and Stengel happened when DiMaggio was hurting and playing this game. He was in center field and all of a sudden here comes Cliff Mapes. Stengel had decided to make a change and he didn't wait until DiMaggio was on the bench. He was going to take him out right off the field. You can't do that to a great star like DiMaggio. He has too much pride. Mapes got to center field and DiMaggio waved him back to the dugout. 'I'll tell Casey when I want to come out.' DiMaggio came to the bench when the inning was over and went right into the clubhouse without a word. I don't think they ever talked again.

"From then on things got worse. Casey couldn't wait until DiMaggio quit. He wanted to get rid of the old guard and get all his own kids in the lineup. He wanted to control every player on the club. Casey wanted one leader on the team—him. When he got there, DiMaggio was the leader. Everybody looked up to him. When we had our meetings for splitting up World Series shares, DiMaggio would decide who would get a full share and who wouldn't. One year we kidded about not giving Casey a full share, but it would have caused too much of a furor."

Rizzuto's account of the bad blood between Stengel and DiMaggio is also borne out by Toots Shor.

"Stengel and Joe never got along good. Stengel just wanted Joe to know that there was only one boss on the Yankees and it would be Casey. I think I remember the day it all started. I looked up at the scoreboard and saw that Joe was batting fifth. If Casey wanted to embarrass him by dropping him down in the lineup, he should have done it on the road, the dirty son of a buck. Casey had Johnny Mize hitting fourth. I started to get up and leave when I saw the lineup. The fans wouldn't have known but the writers would have. They would have written about it.

"Casey never said nothing to Joe. He just put Mize in there against this right-hander and Mize hit two homers. Joe got two hits and came in that night and he's knocking over a belt.

" 'Sore, ain'tcha?'
" 'Yeah, I'm sore. The least he could have done was explain it to me.' "

Jerry Coleman summed up the situation very bluntly: "I really think Casey hated him."

Coleman may have been the most graceful man to play second base in modern times. Watching Phil Rizzuto and Jerry Coleman in the infield was like watching Fred Astaire and Ginger Rogers. Jerry batted .263 for nine seasons with the Yankees, and like so many of his teammates he grew to dislike Stengel for what he considered personal insults to his playing ability. Stengel apparently thought little of Coleman as a hitter and would often bat a pitcher ahead of him in the order, or pinch-hit for him at the earliest opportunity.

"Casey has a large ego and I don't think he liked the idea of anybody on the team being bigger than Casey. Joe was bigger than Casey, bigger than anybody in baseball and most people out of baseball. Casey put DiMaggio at first base one day and that really bothered Joe. He was a man of enormous pride and he knew that he would be embarrassed at playing the strange position. Joe probably could play it. He was a great athlete and could play anywhere, but it isn't that easy to be comfortable at a new position. That move really shook Joe up and I think after one game he told Casey he didn't want to play there again and Casey never put him back on first base.

"One other time Stengel batted Johnny Mize fourth and DiMaggio fifth, and that was a blow to Joe. Joe just felt he was the fourth hitter on the team and when he couldn't do the job he would quit. Casey never told him about it. He just put the card out and that was it. DiMaggio deserved more than that."

It was interesting that complaints against Stengel from Rizzuto, DiMaggio, Coleman, and others mainly concerned lineup changes and position shifts. Perhaps, then, it wasn't Stengel's ego that bothered the players so much as his tactless way of telling them they lacked certain skills or were getting older and couldn't play as well as they once had. Coleman:

"Maybe the angriest I ever saw DiMaggio was in the last week of the 1950 season. We had clinched the pennant and now we were finishing up against the Philadelphia Athletics. Joe had his average just over .300 and he was struggling to keep it there. There were two or three games to go. Stengel asked him if he wanted to sit out the last couple of days, rest up for the Series, and protect his average. Joe would have none of that. He wanted badly to hit a .300, but he wanted to do it playing every game he could. I think he was batting exactly .300 or a point under or a point over. He got up and hit a shot at the shortstop. I'm telling you it could have torn that guy's head off if he wasn't looking. The shortstop was Eddie Joost and he went a couple of feet into the hole and he backhanded that thing with one of the greatest plays I ever saw. Then he straightened up and threw Joe out by an eyelash. It was a terrific play for them. Joe didn't show any emotion on the field but when he got back to the dugout where nobody could see him he exploded. He must have called Joost every name in the book and a few that weren't. He still wound up the season at .301.

"What always impressed me about DiMaggio was his style. He knew instinctively what to do. Once we were playing the Indians when somebody hit a single and tried to get to second on a ground ball I had fielded. I got it to Rizzuto just as the guy arrived and he mashed into Phil and drove him into left field. It was a clean, hard slide. Nothing was said. The next inning Joe singles and is stretching it into a double. Joe Gordon, his old former teammate, was playing second base. Here comes the throw and here comes DiMaggio. He hit Gordon so hard you could hear his bones creak all over the park. He was safe and that was the end of it. Nobody had to spell it out. We were even. That's what I mean by leadership.

"Joe had a way of doing wrong things and making them look right. He once hit a line drive to third base and the third baseman leaped up and made a hell of a catch. There were a couple of men on and Joe was disappointed he hadn't driven them in. Now he comes back to the bench. We used to have a couple of leather bags hanging from a strap in the dugout. One was filled with old balls. The other was empty. DiMaggio came in and he gave one of those leather bags a good swift kick. He thought he was kicking the empty one. Somehow the wrong bag was in the wrong place. He kicked the full bag and he knocked it out of the dugout and the balls went sprawling all over the field. His face got red but we all turned away and nobody moved. We knew how embarrassed he was. I bet if you ask a dozen guys on the bench if they remember that today they'd say they never heard of it. Nobody would want to remember anything that embarrassed DiMaggio. The only reason I remember it is because we got eight or ten runs in the next couple of innings and I think I had four hits that day.

"When I joined the club in '49 we had a lot of young players. Joe DiMaggio didn't know us and we didn't know him. We were dumb and young and didn't know that we weren't supposed to win. The Yankees had finished third in 1948 to the great Cleveland team and to Boston, and we were picked anywhere from third to sixth that season.

"We were making a barnstorming trip through Texas. We got to Fort Worth and all of a sudden DiMaggio was gone. He hadn't said a word to anybody. We thought he had jumped the club for some reason. He had been operated on the previous fall for the bone spur, but he seemed to be coming along. It was only later that we found out the bone spur had kicked up on him again and he was examined by

141

a doctor in Texas. The guy had recommended surgery and Joe went back to Johns Hopkins for another operation.

"It was a pretty upsetting thing for the ball club and we played lousy. We went into Austin for another exhibition game—we were supposed to be working our way north—and we played the Dodgers. Jackie Robinson had a terrific day, had three or four hits and stole home a couple of times, and Stengel went off his rocker. He was shouting at us and telling us to check our lockers to see if we still had our jocks, maybe Robinson stole them too. Anyway, we seemed to wake up after that game and got straightened out by the time we got back to New York. We won eight of the first ten games and seemed to be winning even without DiMaggio.

"Then we began to stagger a little and the Red Sox started to drive and we weren't sure if we could hold them off. We played an exhibition game at the Polo Grounds against the Giants and here was DiMaggio back in the lineup. He just said he woke up one morning and the pain was gone. Things change fast in baseball. Joe played that exhibition game and now he comes back in Boston, hits *four* home runs, and we sweep the series and get straightened out again. That had to be the greatest exhibition of pressure baseball I ever saw."

DiMaggio shocked the country with his incredible display of playing excellence in that series and got more press attention than at any time since his hitting streak. At age thirty-four he had come back from painful surgery to lead the Yankees: a magnificent performance under stress. Coleman recalled the drive against Boston.

"We were all excited by that series. It was a big series for us to knock off the Red Sox, and it was bigger because we knew that we would get some help from DiMaggio the rest of the way. I remember when the last game was over and Joe had helped us win and he was all smiles and he

142

walked by me in the clubhouse and said, 'You can't beat this life, kid.' Nothing made Joe happier than to do well in a big series and help the club win. He was a winner in the finest sense of the word. He was simply the greatest ball-player I ever saw and it's not easy for a man to carry that burden. Joe carried it with class and dignity.

"Things have changed for him. You can see that in him now. Whatever war he fought all these years, he has won it. Joe DiMaggio has come to terms with himself."

Casey Stengel was known as much for his antics as for his play. A nonstop talker, he had a language all his own, later immortalized as "Stengelese." He managed the Yankees for a dozen years, 1949 to 1960, winning five pennants and five World Series in a row, ten pennants and seven Series all told. He was covered in print more than any man who ever handled a baseball team, became an international celebrity, and was forcefully retired by the Yankees after the 1960 season, when he won the pennant but lost the Series to the Pirates. The Yankees said he resigned. Actually, they were retiring him because of his advanced age. At seventy, he was again considered finished, and they paid him handsomely for the privilege of allowing them to bring in Ralph Houk as the new manager.

In 1961 Casey took over the New York Mets and, out of nothing, created a team with a great following.

His house in Glendale, California, is filled with memories of more than six decades of baseball history. There are pictures of Stengel with presidents and kings, baseball stars and politicians, industrialists and actors, and even the emperor of Japan. Having traveled to Japan a number of times to play exhibitions, he is as well known in downtown Tokyo as he is in New York.

At eighty-four, Stengel is as crisp of mind as he was more than sixty years ago when he first entered baseball. His face seems chiseled out of a block of concrete, more suitable for Mount Rushmore than for a living man. His hair is thin and a sort of burnt orange, in tribute to the dozens of different preparations he has used to keep it from being white. He walks with a small waddle, the result of bad outfields, cracked knees, and a broken hip late in life. (His hip is held to his leg by a steel ball.) He drinks bourbon, and every time he takes a shot he breaks his own lifetime record. He has never been known to get inebriated, despite the gargantuan quantity of spirits he has consumed in more than seventy years of participation. "When he dies," Pitcher Johnny Murphy once said of him, "they'll have to send his liver to the Smithsonian."

About Joe DiMaggio?

"Now wait a minute, for crissakes. You're going into too big a man. He coulda been anything, he was so good. Maybe he woulda been an astronaut if he wanted it. Why wouldn't he want to hit some balls off the moon and see if they'd carry? I can't say he was the greatest ever because I'm saving that for my book. There were a lot of great ones and Ruth could pitch too, and a lot of them could play the wall and run and throw.

"About DiMaggio you don't have to falsify anything. He started in with a bang and never stopped. Of course, when he played for me he was handicapped but you wouldn'ta knowed it if you didn't see him limping in the clubhouse and the cabs when he went home. He tried to play every day and sometimes he could and you wouldn't want him to because maybe you had five outfielders and you could rest him a day and save him for another series and what would be wrong about that.

"He didn't talk much but he didn't have to talk because he could execute. A lot of them talk a lot and tell you how good they are until you see them play on the field and the pitcher throws a curve ball and they don't hit it and now they come back to the bench and curl up and sit real quiet like, hoping you didn't notice that they didn't get it. Especially them that never moves the bat and takes, whoops, strike one, whoops, strike two, whoops, strike three, and you can't improve your average with your bat upon your shoulder, tra la, tra la, tra la.

"The best thing about him is that he wasn't trying to learn swimming so he didn't dive after any fly balls. He would come in fast and just get under the ball or catch it on his shoes, bending down without doing a couple of flops or hoping maybe it would hit him in the glove like a lot of them do. And what if you catch it and you hit the ground on the dive and it goes out, whoops, and now everybody's running all around the bases and you have a six-run inning because the man left his feet?

"When I had him you didn't have to look at center field and see he was lined up. He knew how to line up right. The others looked at him. If he moved, they moved. If he stood there, they stood there. Then we got Mantle and he didn't say anything, just stuck out his jaw and looked at DiMaggio. Mantle was in right field and DiMaggio would wave his hand at him a little and Mantle would move over and all of a sudden here would come the ball and he'd catch it and everybody would say what a smart young outfielder, he knows exactly where to play. Only thing is nobody remembered to move him in the World Series, and he fell in that hole and couldn't run the same after that.

"The best thing DiMaggio had—I'll give you a tip—was his head. He saw some of the faults the pitcher had and he would hit the ball, and he didn't hit it just on Sunday neither. He hit it whenever they threw it and he hit it all over the park and over the wall a lot for you too. He was flawless on the bases too, and when he couldn't throw he would fool you because he would catch the ball when you thought it was a single or a double.

"What do you mean did I get along with him? I played him, didn't I? One time I played him at first base and that was a mistake, but why wouldn't you play him there when his legs were getting older and you had five other outfielders who could go out there and play good? Everybody looked at him in center field even if they had big names in right field and left field. They said I didn't like him but every time I saw him my wife, Edna, would say hello to him and give me a poke and I would say hello. You don't have to say hello a lot if a man can play flawless like DiMaggio.

"He could hit the ball and he wasn't afraid of the pitcher, even if he would throw it close at his neck or something. He didn't have to run out to the pitcher's box and stand there looking at him like some dummy or mummy. He would just stand at the plate and hit the next one over a building or maybe just hit a line drive that would hurt the third baseman's hands, and that would be enough for the pitcher to stop trying to make him get in the dirt when he had a clean uniform and didn't want to get in the dirt.

"If you had to say what was the biggest thing he could do in life, you would say it would be to execute every play they ever had in the field, at the plate, or on the bases, like fellows who run faster but not better. What about his arm? He could go up to Boston and play twenty-seven of them off the wall and get twenty-seven assists and everybody would say, oh, what a wonderful day that pitcher had, he got everybody out before they got to second base, but nobody would say that it was Mr. DiMaggio that got them out for you.

"Then he could bunt too, and those big fellows sometimes won't do it for you because they want to hit a ball off a wall and if you're bunting it won't go that far. What was wrong with Rizzuto bunting because he was a little fellow, and then DiMaggio bunted with Rizzuto together and the one man scored from third and the other was safe on first base and we won the pennant with them, so the bunt didn't look bad in the box scores? You would think some of the others would practice that play but they wanted to hit the ball off walls and a lot of them didn't make that good a living. DiMaggio did and he would practice the bunt and do it for you if he wanted to win a game.

"You hafta say that if you got into a game with the Yankees in them days and you had to win it, there was a lot of ways you could win it with Mr. DiMaggio. For one, you could win it with a hit if it was the first inning or the seventh, and not a lot of them can do that. For another, he could throw you out with a bum shoulder when a lot of them couldn't scare you even though the crowd would go ooh and aah because it was hard, but it might also bounce off a rail and it's a hard play to throw a man out off a rail. What about catching the ball if it was going into the bullpen or hit in front of the man? Don't you think he could do that for you even if his legs were all wrapped up and he had a sore knee? What if he went from second to third when a lot of them wouldn't because the ball was in left field and you aren't supposed to do it except if you know you can make it like DiMaggio and you did?

"Now wait a minute, I could tell you a lot more things. There were a lot of people who could play ball that I saw, and DiMaggio could as good as any of them, but I can't tell you who was the best because the others would all get angry and some of them are already dead at the present time.

"I'm not going to tell you everything because you have to have room for what those other fellows tell you, but I'll

147

tell you one thing—there wasn't nothing in baseball DiMaggio couldn't do with his head or his body. He was rather splendid in his line of work."

Ralph Houk, the bullpen catcher and third-stringer behind Berra and Charlie Silvera, was a good friend of DiMaggio's.

"I was just a kid, a busher, when I joined the Yankees and Joe DiMaggio was nice to me. He talked to me, kidded with me; he helped me along. You can imagine what a thrill that was. He gave me words of encouragement all along the line. Without a doubt, Joe was one of the greatest leaders in the history of baseball.

"We would go out to dinner together a lot and it was hard to eat with him. There were always people coming over in every town in the league. You tried to be nice to them but it was hard. They just wouldn't let him alone. Everyone knew him. He just had an immediately recognizable face and there was no place for him to hide. He signed what autographs he could and hoped people would leave him alone.

"He never really complained about that. He never complained about anything. Even in 1949, when he had the bad heel and couldn't play, he never moaned. He just worked hard every day at trying to get ready. When he did, that was the greatest show I ever saw. Here's a guy coming out of an operation, no spring training, goes in against the best pitching in baseball and tears the cover off the ball. That was some exhibition of guts.

"See, the thing that made Joe tick was winning. That's all he cared about. He was a winner. He didn't care what he did personally as long as the team won. When we lost and he had four hits, he was really down. He was just a great team player. The only thing you can really say about Joe now is the same as we all said then: he just has a hell of a lot of greatness in him. He still has the greatest respect from anybody who sees him. I never saw him do anything wrong. I never heard a bad story about him, not one, in all the years I played with him. That's almost unbelievable for a guy that was in baseball as long as Joe."

Mel Allen, the Voice of the Yankees, stood in the October sunshine, a microphone in front of him at home plate. His voice rose sharply, the Alabama drawl becoming more pronounced. He paused for an instant, took a deep breath, and studied some of the nearby faces in the huge crowd of nearly seventy thousand people. Then he leaned forward and spoke slowly, letting his words echo back to him through the cavernous Yankee Stadium.

"Ladies and gentlemen . . . boys and girls . . . here he is . . ." The noise began to swell through the stands. ". . . The Yankee Clipper!"

Thousands were shouting and applauding and stomping their feet on the concrete, whistling, screaming. "Joltin' Joe Di-Mag-gio!"

Joe D was coming from the top step of the dugout now, a long, lithe figure in a loose-fitting white pinstriped uniform, the number five on his shirt billowing as he jogged gracefully toward home plate, his head down, his eyes on the grass. He had taken half a dozen soft steps and now his eyes caught his mother's and he lifted his head higher and removed his cap, waving to his right and to his left as the roar of the crowd rocked the old stadium.

He hugged his mother, shook hands with his brother, slapped the backs of his teammates, and stared wanly at the assortment of wealth collected in front of him to mark Joe DiMaggio day, 1949, in the custom of the times— $7,197 collected by his fans for Joe to turn over to a charity, a Cadillac, a Dodge, a motorboat, cheese from Wisconsin, a four-year college scholarship for anyone he selected, 300 quarts of ice cream, some television sets, radios, phonographs, 300 free taxi rides, hand painted ties and a cocker spaniel his son later named "Yankee Clipper."

Joe's face was lean and long, the Roman nose dominating. Around the edges of his hair were flecks of gray.

The tumult lasted some four minutes, and suddenly the ball park grew still. He stood in front of the microphone and held his cap at his side, his hand trembling slightly, his face set.

"When I was in San Francisco," he began, a slight crack in his voice, "Lefty O'Doul told me, 'Joe, don't let the big city scare you. New York is the friendliest town in the world.' This day proves it. I want to thank my fans . . . my friends . . . my manager, Casey Stengel . . . my teammates—the gamest, fightingest bunch of guys that ever lived." His voice was again confident and deep. "And I want to thank the good Lord for making me a Yankee."

14: The Stretch

In his next-to-last year Joe DiMaggio was playing with young, talented rookies who, he knew, would see many more seasons than he had left. Billy Martin, a flamboyant and controversial second baseman, was one of them.

"It was the first day of spring training in 1950, over in St. Petersburg. I had played a couple of years in the Coast League and now I was getting a chance to make the big club. Stengel had been my manager at Oakland and he liked me there. He was the manager of the Yankees now so I thought I had a good shot at making the team.

"The workout was over on the first day and DiMaggio comes up to me in front of a lot of the other players and says, 'Let's have dinner tonight together, kid.' I don't know why he did it. I guess maybe he knew I was Italian like him and from Berkeley and he just liked me. He had probably heard a little bit about me before I came to the camp.

"It shook up the whole clubhouse. Me too. There were a lot of guys who had been on the team for years who had never had dinner with him. We went out to some Italian place that night, had a couple of beers later, and became friends. The next day the guys kidded me about it—about being Joe's little bobo. I teased them pretty good too. I told them Joe knew class when he saw it. That's why he invited me out.

"After that we were together a lot. We'd go some place and then walk in the clubhouse together and the guys would kid me and call me Joe's bobo and ask me if I was going to shine his shoes and things like that. We just got along good. I treated him like an equal. I could kid him. When Joe walked into the Yankee clubhouse it was like a senator or the President of the United States walking into a room. All eyes would turn toward him. He'd walk by and one guy would say, 'Hi, Joe,' and Joe would say, 'Hi, kid,' and that would continue down the line. 'Hi, Joe.' 'Hi, kid.' 'Hi, Joe.' 'Hi, kid.' Then he would walk over to me and say, 'Hi, Dago,' and I would say to him, 'Hi, kid.'

"I always liked to imitate him a lot. It used to break him up. I did it when he was around and I did it when he wasn't around. Joe used to come in and go to his locker and take his pants off and hang them up. Never his shirt first, always his pants. Then he'd call over to the clubhouse guy, Pete Sheehy, and say, 'Hey, Pete, half a cup of coffee.' Sometimes I'd come in, go to my locker, take my pants off, and yell, 'Hey, Pete, half a cup of coffee.' He wanted to throw it at me.

"After a while we started palling around on the road. I always rooted like mad for him. If he didn't get any hits and we lost, we ate in his room. If he had a big day and we won, we would go out. I was a young kid then. I wanted to go out all the time. I wanted to see what was out there.

"The winter after I played with Joe I went home and nobody would believe that Joe was my good friend. I had to tell things about going out with him and having dinner with him or being together with him some place before they really would accept the idea that I was friendly with the great Joe D.

"People ask my why Joe was attracted to me. And I can't answer it. Maybe opposites attract. I always felt protective of him. I always felt you had to keep some people away from him. He is so recognizable that it's easy to annoy him in public. I guess he liked me because I was always willing to do the things he wanted to do.

"I see Joe once in a while now. He's like a big brother to me. I remember when my wife and I were married and we were having dinner in a restaurant in Chicago. Here comes DiMaggio. He was so gracious—gave me this big hello. Gretchen was really impressed. She kept saying, 'Isn't it great that Joe DiMaggio would come over and say hello to us?' Joe was always like that. If you were his friend he made a fuss over you. You didn't have to make a fuss over him.

"Joe was Mr. Perfection. His last year was a tough time for him. He was hitting a lot of balls to right and right center that he used to pull to left. Even if he hit a home run to the right side he wasn't happy. He used to call them piss home runs and he would say, 'I could piss them over that wall. That's not hitting.' He couldn't pull because his back was bothering him. Remember that stance he had, his arms held up high over his head and stretched out real far? Well, he couldn't do that at the end; he couldn't whip the bat. His back hurt him and he just couldn't get his arms up high and swing right.

"One thing about Joe that I didn't agree with. He wasn't too crazy about Casey. I think he resented the way Casey treated him at the end. It was a tough situation. I don't know if anybody could have handled it. I don't know if that had any bearing on Joe quitting but it didn't help. He quit because he couldn't play any more and he was too proud to just hang on. In '51 he saw Mickey for the first time and he knew the greatness in him. There was no jealousy and he recognized that Mickey was somebody special. Any guy who could hit a baseball five hundred feet with each hand had to be something special. There's never been anybody like that.

"He told me he was quitting in the middle of '51 and I got his last bat and his last pair of spikes and a couple of his jerseys. I keep all that stuff in a special place in my home. I look at it all the time. The bat was covered with olive oil. He used to rub the oil into it to keep it smooth. He would sit there and just rub and rub and rub. The spikes are interesting too. He had that heel trouble and both spikes were built up to ease the pressure on his feet. I don't know how the man played. He really must have been hurting at the end."

Whitey Ford was four lockers away from Joe DiMaggio at the spring-training camp that same year. He was twenty-one then. Twenty-four years later the witty and popular Yankee pitcher would be elected to the Hall of Fame, along with his teammate Mickey Mantle. That spring he was just another rookie awed by the great DiMag.

"I was afraid to talk to him. Billy Martin was a rookie that year and they talked like old friends. I couldn't do something like that. I wanted to see if I could make the club first. Billy didn't worry about things like that. He wasn't afraid of anybody.

"I remember the first time I saw Joe in the clubhouse. I

153

had this crazy thought. When I was going to junior high school and high school, we had this baseball pool going and I was the bookmaker. You would give a kid three players and they had to get six hits for a win. We paid five-to-one odds if they got six hits. The biggest bet was probably a dime or a quarter. Anyway, about three-quarters of the guys would take DiMaggio every day. The rest of them would take Williams. There were days when DiMaggio would get three or four hits and he would wipe me out.

"I started out with Binghamton. Lefty Gomez was my first manager. I pitched about five weeks and he sent me out to Butler, Pennsylvania. [Says Gomez, "I'm the only manager in history to send Whitey Ford out. It shows you how smart I was."] Then I worked my way up and came to the Yankees in 1950. I didn't make the club in the spring but I got off good and they recalled me on July 3, 1950.

"We were behind about 12–2 when Casey sent me into the game to mop up. I couldn't find the plate and I got killed. The final score was 17–4 or something like that. After that I only pitched against second-division teams for a month. Then I started doing better. We were tied for the lead and Casey started me against Detroit. Dizzy Trout was pitching for Detroit. Then DiMaggio homers in the top of the fifth and I'm leading 1–0. In the bottom of the eighth Jerry Priddy and Vic Wertz hit line-drive doubles back to back off me and the score is tied. I figured I was gone. But Casey kept me in and I got the next three guys out on ground balls.

"Now it's the top of the ninth and I'm scheduled as the first hitter. I figured I was gone for sure and I look around and Casey is looking off in some other direction so I go up there and hit. Trout must have heard what a good hitter I was in sandlot ball so he was afraid of me. He surprised the whole ball park and walked me. Then there was a sacrifice and another walk and DiMaggio is up. He hits a line-drive single to score me and we win the game 2–1 and stay in first place the rest of the season.

"The next day I pick up the papers and there it is in big, black headlines: 'FORD AND DIMAGGIO BEAT TIGERS.' If you think that wasn't something. I must have bought fifty of those papers that day and sent them all home.

"Then we got into the World Series against Philadelphia and I got to start the fourth game. We were leading 5–0 with two out in the ninth and Gene Woodling dropped a fly ball and two runs scored. Stengel came to the mound, took the ball, and brought in Reynolds. I was really mad. I wanted to finish my first World Series game but Casey knew best. Reynolds came in, threw three pitches, struck out Stan Lopata, and the World Series was over.

"I play golf with Joe every spring in Florida. We play in a couple of tournaments down there, the Jackie Gleason Inverrary and a couple of others. He's a real good golfer, has a real good long game, but he has a little trouble putting. He kids around a lot with me and Mickey and Billy and all of us. He's real relaxed with us and with everybody around. He has a lot of fun and he's fun to be with. When it's all over we all sit down and have a beer. It's still a thrill to sit down and have a beer with Joe DiMaggio."

15: The Last Season

In the spring of 1951 the Yankees, at the urging of Casey Stengel, established an early training camp. They had switched training sites that year with the New York Giants and were training in Phoenix while the Giants trained in St. Petersburg. Stengel referred to his early training camp as his "instructural school." Three young men were to become Yankees as a result of that early training camp:

Mickey Mantle, pitcher Tom Morgan and infielder Gil McDougald.

Gil McDougald is an executive now, with his own business in New Jersey. He also coaches the baseball team at Fordham University.

"Joe was in his final year. Everybody knew he was quitting. He had told a few people in the spring it would be his last year. That kind of word gets around. I didn't talk to him much. He seemed beyond approach. Somehow or other you just shied away from him. He was such an important person in baseball. It was as if you were playing with somebody you had only read about in storybooks. I remember once after we came East we played the Giants in an exhibition game. I was still fighting for a job and I was batting in front of DiMaggio. The pitcher was Sal Maglie and he was about as tough as they come. DiMaggio just watched Maglie warm up and came up to me. 'He hasn't got shit today.' I just went up to the plate with confidence and hit the first pitch for a hard single. I felt if I didn't do it I would have embarrassed DiMaggio.

"We were traveling on the train in the middle of the season and I was sitting with Rizzuto and DiMaggio came up to us with a few business envelopes in his hands. They were from different companies that wanted to make deals with Joe. 'I wish I could give you guys these offers.' He really felt badly that people wanted to sign him for this deal and that deal and he couldn't talk them into taking some of the other guys on the club. He wanted to share the wealth.

"In a way the season was a little sad for Joe. You wished he would go out with a really big year. Instead, all anybody talked about was Mantle. He was hitting those incredible home runs all over Arizona and California and he was the big thunder that spring. Joe wasn't getting around on the ball. He was worried. You could see that. He didn't want to embarrass himself or the ball club. He was a man of such incredible pride. He had pride in everything he did in the game—hitting, running, fielding, throwing—a complete player. I try to teach my kids that here at Fordham. Pride is hard to instill in a kid. It's something he really has to do for himself.

"Joe always had great feeling for other people. He was a little self-conscious about showing it when he played. He doesn't seem to be that way now. I enjoy him more now. I was with him in Fort Lauderdale last year and we worked together filming one of those commercials of his for the Bowery Savings Bank. I was in it with Joe and Elston Howard and Tommy Henrich. Joe was like the professional actor with a bunch of amateurs. We had a good time doing it. I think those commercials have been a terrific thing for him. It always helps an old ballplayer in business if people know you are still alive."

Two Yankees, Gene Woodling and Hank Bauer, typify Casey Stengel's era with the Yankees. They were *platooned* players. Stengel did not invent platoon baseball; he himself had been a platooned player in his own time. He simply refined it, making it a vital part of his managerial system. He felt it used a player's ability to full advantage and that he could get more production out of a position by filling it with two men, often of very equal or similar abilities.

Gene Woodling was the left-handed-hitting part of the best platoon. A stocky outfielder with marvelous bat control and occasional long-ball power, Woodling played for the Indians and Pirates before coming to the Yankees in 1949. He was a key part of the Yankee teams that were to win five straight championships. He and Bauer were listed as an entry. A strong-willed man, bright, articulate, and outspoken, Woodling battled Stengel for all the time he

157

was on the Yankees, over Casey's decision to pair him with Bauer. He bristled at the thought that he couldn't hit left-handed pitching after recording some incredible batting marks in the minor leagues.

"Joe DiMaggio was a fantastic name to me. I was just starting in baseball when he had that hitting streak. That was the most unbelievable thing. Golly, it was a real thrill to join the Yankees and play with him. My Lord, it really would have been disgraceful if they didn't name him the all-time greatest living player. It was no contest. He simply was the best there was.

"I was fairly friendly with Joe when we played together. I roomed with Ralph Houk, and Ralph was close to Joe. Sometimes the three of us would go out to dinner together on the road. Joe was a professional there too. He always reached for the check.

"He helped me a lot in the outfield when I came to the Yankees. I played left field most of the time, next to him, and the rule always is to let the center fielder catch any ball he can get his hands on. Joe watched me for a while and then he came up to me one day and said, 'Your left side is your strong side. Go get those balls to your left. Don't worry about me. I won't run into you.' He realized that he had slowed down a bit and he wanted to do what was best for the team. So I began shading a little more to center field, and I bet a lot of balls in those deep spots in left center field in the stadium were caught by me or Joe because we understood each other's range.

"Joe never got into that thing with Hank and me about the platooning business. It was really overplayed anyway. There were a lot of games where Hank and I played together. Casey just believed in using the best three guys out there on that particular day. Sometimes it depended on the pitcher or the park or the weather or whatever. Casey always had a reason. He knew why he was doing it. We screamed a lot about platooning. Every ballplayer wants to play every day. If he doesn't, he shouldn't be out there in the first place. I think it had a lot to do with our winning. We pulled hard for each other on that team. There were no jealousies. The idea was to win and make that money for all of us. We were outspoken, and when the press asked us what we thought about platooning we told them. The old man enjoyed every minute of it. He liked to see us standing up for our rights. We were important guys on that team and we didn't like sitting, but we didn't pout. We just sat on the bench and pulled for each other.

"The '49 season was my first with the Yankees and the two biggest things that year were DiMaggio's comeback in June in Boston and those last two games of the season. He was sick and he played and we won both games and we won the pennant. Johnny Lindell hit a home run and we knew we had it after that. We were behind and we came back and nobody was going to catch the Yankees in a big game like that once we got ahead.

"Joe was slowing down a bit when I got there but he was still the best outfielder in baseball. He made up, with his knowledge of the game, for what he lacked in running speed. Pure speed doesn't do much good if you don't know how to use it. Nobody used running speed the way DiMaggio did on the bases or in the field. He just had that incredible knack, that timing, that second sense that separates the great players from the average players. The good Lord gives you a certain amount of abilities. It is up to each man to use those abilities in the very best way he can. Baseball is no different than farming or anything else for that matter. If you use what you have to the best of your ability, you'll always make out in this world.

"I run into Joe here and there now, and he loves to kid about the old days. That's why I enjoy those Old Timers' Days so much. It's just fun to sit around and see and talk to all the guys and think about what we were all like when we were younger. It's good that the Yankees think of us now and invite us all back. I think baseball tradition is really a big part of the game, and it's important to have that link with the past and show the young players that they are playing for a proud team and a proud record as much as they are playing for themselves. The Yankees had some squabbles among themselves, like all ball clubs, but they really pulled together against the other teams. Those years were the happiest years I had in baseball and I'm still proud to have been part of it."

Hank Bauer was the other half of the Stengel outfield platoon. Someone once said, "He has a face like a clenched fist." No man seemed tougher, stronger, more rugged, more certain of his strength than Bauer. He played baseball with an incredible intensity, challenging the pitch at bat, attacking walls, fighting for every hit. He was and is a man's man, a leader. Like most ex-marines, he seems never to have been separated from the corps.

Bauer joined the Yankees in 1948, played with them through 1959, managed the Baltimore Orioles to a World Series championship in 1966, managed in the minor leagues for the Mets and retired after the 1972 season. He now owns and operates Hank's Liquor Store in Prairie Village, Kansas, not far from where he was born and began his career. On Saturday mornings Bauer rests comfortably at home with his wife and perhaps one or more of their four grown children. He still sports the crewcut he has favored for three decades. His appearance is still rugged and he is, even at fifty-two, not a man to tangle with.

"I came up in '48 and there was this off day in Washington. We were staying at the Shoreham Hotel and I was rooming with Spec Shea. The Shoreham had this real nice patio out back and we went out there to have lunch. The sun was shining and the band was playing and it was really pleasant to sit out there and listen to them. We ordered a highball and were listening to the music. DiMaggio came out from the lobby and sat down on the other side of the patio. We saw him but we didn't bother him. We knew that DiMaggio liked to be alone a lot. Then he looked over at us and waved for us to join him. We went over, had another drink with him, had some lunch, and listened to the music. Then it was time to go and the check came. I was making seven thousand dollars then, but I wasn't going to have anybody buy me anything. DiMaggio grabbed the check. 'When you eat with the Dago, the Dago pays.' He just wouldn't ever let you pick up a check.

"It was a miracle, I guess, that I was even there. It didn't seem like I would ever make it to the big leagues. In 1941 I had signed with the Yankees and been sent to Grand Forks, North Dakota, to play. In January 1942 I enlisted in the Marines and was with Jimmy Roosevelt's outfit for thirty-four months. My brother was in the Army and he was killed in France. He had been drafted and sent over there right away. I was in the South Pacific. I was in Okinawa for a week and I was hit. Then I was in the hospital for a while so they could pull the shrapnel out of me and I was back on the lines. I think I was there a week before I was hit again. All in all I had three or four bronze stars and the purple heart and made all those islands. The war ended and they sent me to Japan. I played a little ball there. I hadn't played for about four years and I was catching in my first game against this colored team. A guy hit a foul ball and it broke two of my fingers. You could see why I wasn't much interested in baseball.

"I went home after that and got a job as an iron worker in this mill for three bucks an hour. That was pretty good money in those days and I figured I would be an iron worker the rest of my life. I didn't want to play ball any more. I

161

had enough of that traveling around in the Marines. I just wanted to stay home. There was this tavern near where I was working in East St. Louis, Illinois, and the guy that ran it knew my brother. He had a baseball team and he asked me to play with his team. I weighed a hundred and two pounds then. I had really been wiped out by that malaria I had contracted in the South Pacific.

"After a while the scouts started coming around and watching our games. This guy came up to me and asked me if I wanted to play again. He said they would pay me a hundred and seventy-five bucks a month and give me a two-hundred-dollar bonus if I signed to play again. I don't know why I decided to take it but I did. Maybe I was getting tired of pushing iron around. Anyway, I went to Quincy, Illinois, to play in the Three I League. I was a catcher then. Frank Lane was running that club and he switched me to the outfield. I guess he saw my hands and figured a few more broken fingers and that would be it for baseball. I did pretty good there after a while. I led the club in hitting and the Yankees promoted me to Kansas City in 1947. We were tied for the pennant on the last day of the season and we lost it to Alvin Dark's team. The Yankees didn't invite me to spring training in 1948 and I thought about quitting then. I was twenty-six and I figured that maybe they thought I was too old to take a chance on me. Then they called me up late in 1948.

"Joe helped me a lot when I first went to the Yankees. He helped you just by being there. He also helped in the outfield, wiggling his glove this way or that so you moved on the different hitters. He always knew the hitters. He did it in such a way that the fans never realized he was moving you around, because DiMaggio never would do anything that would embarrass anybody else. He didn't want the fans to think that you didn't know how to play a certain hitter.

162

"I'll never forget my first time up in the stadium. My knees were shaking. This time it wasn't from malaria. I was just damn scared. Snuffy Stirnweiss had doubled and Henrich had popped up. Now I was up and Stirnweiss started to steal third on his own. I didn't see it. I was watching the pitch. I swung and hit a line drive right at him. It missed him by a hair and that scared me even more. I don't know what would have happened if I had beaned a guy with my first swing in the big leagues.

"After a while I got settled down there and started to play pretty good. Stengel came in '49 and we were winning every year after that. Guys played hard and pulled together, and we had a hell of a lot of talent on those clubs. DiMaggio was terrific in '49 after that injury and he still could play good after that year. I think he could have played another year or two if he had wanted to, if he had decided to stay on.

"We kind of got used to going to the bank every November with those big World Series checks. Once in a while a guy didn't hustle and we had a way of making sure he did his job. We'd get him in the clubhouse, two or three of us, and remind him that we expected to get those checks every year and if he wasn't hustling he was cheating us out of our money. We would have to remind a guy to quit fooling with our money. DiMaggio never said anything to anybody about not hustling. He'd just look at you. That was enough. Nobody wanted to risk DiMaggio's displeasure. If Joe looked at a guy like he was unhappy about something, that guy would really bust his ass after that. It must have been a good system because we kept winning."

"Certain pitchers were getting Joe out with the slider," said Eddie Lopat, "and he felt bad about it. He knew he just couldn't handle the pitch. They took him out a couple of times and gave him a rest but it didn't help. He just couldn't play like he used to. He was in a lot of pain and his back and his shoulder and his leg were bothering him. One day in August he just walked by after a tough game and said, 'I don't think I can stand it any more.'

"You never really think of a great player like that ever quitting. Somehow you think guys like that can go on forever. I don't know why that is but it is. Everybody knows the end will come, but you don't ever think it will come for guys like DiMaggio."

The inevitable was obvious to Jerry Coleman too.

"You could see that he didn't have it any more. He had one throw a game from the outfield, and he didn't have the snap in his bat like he did before. He must have hit ten doubles that shook the chalk on the right-field foul line. They were hits but he wasn't proud of them. He wanted every hit to be a hard rocket to the left side. He had to be a perfectionist, even in the hits he got. Me, I hit some bloops that thrilled me.

A seriousness edged into Phil Rizzuto's voice as he talked about Joe's last year.

"I used to watch him and it was agony for him just getting in and out of a taxicab. When I first came up Joe was so good he could tell you he was going to handcuff the third baseman with a hot grounder and go out and do it. He had such great pride in himself. It was a beautiful thing to watch Joe against Bobby Feller. Joe loved to match his strength against Feller's. When he couldn't do that any more, when he started to hit balls to right field that he should have been pulling to left, he knew it was time."

One evening DiMaggio turned to veteran *New York Times* photographer Ernie Sisto and told his friend that he was retiring soon. Sisto sadly asked why. Joe replied: "Because I don't want them to remember me struggling."

16: Hanging It Up

The official announcement of the end of the brilliant playing career of Joe DiMaggio came on December 11, 1951, after the Yankees had won the championship again by defeating the Giants in the World Series. A press conference was called for the Yankee office in the Squibb Tower building on Fifth Avenue in Manhattan. Shortly before two o'clock Arthur "Red" Patterson, the publicity man of the New York Yankees, walked into a room crowded with reporters, photographers, and radio and television men. He handed out printed sheets to all the waiting reporters. DiMaggio, Casey Stengel, and George Weiss, along with owners Dan Topping and Del Webb, stood off to the side of the room. The release was short and to the point. "Joe DiMaggio today announced his retirement as an active player." It went on to recite all of DiMaggio's heroics and listed his statistical records. There was no way of listing or recording the enormous impact DiMaggio had made on baseball, on the city, on the country.

"Why are you quitting?" a reporter shouted.

"I no longer have it," DiMaggio replied quietly.

It was an honest and direct statement. DiMaggio elaborated on the answer by citing his advancing age and wounded body, the advent of night baseball, the increased skills of young pitchers.

DiMaggio touched the high points and the few low points of his career. He said physical injuries were his major problem and talked about the possibilities of future employment. He seemed relieved that the decision he had made nearly a year earlier had finally been announced publicly.

Stengel was restrained. "What is there to say? I just gave

165

the big guy's glove away to the Hall of Fame." All the anger between Stengel and DiMaggio seemed spent. It was over now and only the greatness of the man would remain. "He was the greatest player I ever managed," said Stengel.

DiMaggio admitted that the decision had been delayed at the request of the owners, Webb and Topping, but had really been irrevocable.

"I knew my mind was made up after the World Series," he said, "but I was asked to think it over, so in fairness to Topping I thought about it a little while longer. I never mentioned it to another soul."

The questions came for another few minutes. Then there was nothing more to say.

The afternoon event was soon over. DiMaggio sat in Topping's office for some few minutes, smoking and talking softly with his friend and boss, certain he had made this important decision correctly. Then he left and with two sportswriter friends walked the four blocks to Toots Shor's place.

It is a quarter of a century since DiMaggio left the playing fields, yet so many people remember his career. No one who ever saw Joe DiMaggio glide back for a fly ball, hit a line drive, or race from first to third on a routine single to left could ever forget.

Del Webb died on July 4, 1974.* When interviewed, he was still active as president of the Del E. Webb Corporation, commuting almost daily in his private plane between Phoenix and Los Angeles. He was a tall, thin man, partially bald, with thick glasses, casual and friendly. An industrial giant with interests in construction and development, real estate, and assorted business ventures, he had built apartment complexes and developments in California, Arizona, Florida,

---

* His partner, Dan Topping, passed away a few months earlier, on May 18.

and other resort areas. In 1951 he was also the co-owner of the New York Yankees.

"Yes, I love to talk about Joe DiMaggio. He's the finest gentleman I ever knew in baseball. A great asset to the game. It's very sad that he didn't stay in baseball. I don't know all the details of why it happened but baseball should have kept DiMaggio around. He is a giant of the game and there are so few people of that stature around any more.

"Why, it was only last year that I was invited to a testimonial dinner in San Francisco for Joe. I don't remember what the sponsorship was—some kind of charity. That's about the only thing that gets Joe out. Every big name in baseball was there. Joe McCarthy came all the way out from New York to the dinner because he wanted to honor Joe. He's quite old now, eighty-six or eighty-seven, but he wanted to be there. There were a dozen or more speeches. Then they called on McCarthy to say a few words. He stood up, looked at the audience and at Joe. There were tears in his eyes. He said, 'Joe was one ballplayer who never made a mental mistake.' That's all he said. He sat down. The crowd stood up and gave McCarthy a standing ovation that must have lasted two minutes.

"Joe had a great year and we offered him this terrific bonus deal. He would have made a hundred thirty, a hundred forty thousand dollars. That's 1948 we're talking about, and that was a great deal of money. Well, Joe let Toots Shor talk him out of that and he took the one-hundred-thousand-dollar straight deal and that's all there was to that.

"Then Joe's heel began bothering him a lot and he had to have that operation. The doctor did a lousy job, and he didn't recover. He was trying to play on that soft sand in Texas in the spring of '49 and it was killing him. The heel began swelling up like nobody's business. He left the club and I took him to this doctor I knew in Dallas. He ordered

167

a special shoe made for Joe to relieve some of the pressure on his foot.

"While we were in his house—Joe and I—the doctor decided to take X-rays of his back. He thought maybe the problems of the heel might be caused by some deformity in the back, the way he walked or the pressure he was putting on his heel. So he wheeled out all this fancy X-ray equipment. Then he said to me, 'I'd like to X-ray your back at the same time.' I told him there was nothing wrong with my back, that I was feeling fine and we were here to see what he could do for Joe. He said that was why he wanted to X-ray my back. He said he wanted to take a picture of Joe's back and then take a picture of mine and show them both to us for comparison.

"Now he takes these pictures and we both think it's silly but we go along with it. Sure enough, the pictures did show something. The doctor had them up on the wall and he's showing us the difference in the two X-rays. He's holding *mine* and he says that this is a picture of an athlete's back, and now he's holding Joe's and he says *that* is the picture of an older man with arthritis. The doctor felt that Joe had a bad back, was developing serious arthritis, and would have a lot of trouble with his back in the next few years. He was right too. Joe did have a lot of trouble. He couldn't stand up straight at the plate after a while and that probably was as important a reason for Joe quitting as anything else.

"We won the pennant in '49, '50, and '51. Joe had mentioned to Topping and me that he was thinking of quitting early in '51, but we didn't want him to think about it until after the season was over. He was dropping hints all around that spring that it would be his last year, but we wanted him to wait and see. We figured if he had a good season he might change his mind. Especially if he felt good. He didn't press the point early in the year and we didn't press him.

168

"Joe didn't have a good year in '51. We could see that he was hurting. There were stories in the papers that Joe was having a busy nightlife, hitting all the clubs, going out a lot, and that was supposed to be the reason he wasn't doing well. The papers said he was tired all the time and he was looking bad and they tried to blame it all on going out. That had nothing to do with it at all. Joe was going to bed early. The problem was he couldn't sleep. He was in too much pain, from his back, his heel, his knees, just about everything.

"One day he came up to Topping's apartment after the World Series was over. He said, 'I'm never going to put that goddamn uniform on again. Nobody knows how much pain I've been in. I'm finished. I can't play any more.' Well, Topping and I figured maybe it was just a little emotional and physical exhaustion, and we asked him to go home to San Francisco for a month or so, rest up, and think about it a little more. We told him we would give him a contract for the same money in 1952 and we actually had it drawn up. Joe went home but we knew it was a losing battle. He was hurting a lot and he just didn't want to come back as a part-time player. He had enormous pride. If he couldn't play ball the way people expected Joe DiMaggio to play ball, then he was going to end it. He just wouldn't come back so he could take the money. He had to earn every penny we paid him.

"He called us a few weeks later, said that nothing had changed, told us he would be quitting for sure and any time we wanted to announce it to the press would be fine with him. We set a date and that was it. He came in and announced to the press that he was quitting and it was over. I don't think anybody was surprised. He hadn't played well that year and it just seemed logical that he would quit and not just hang on. Joe DiMaggio wouldn't just go out there for a dollar. He was too proud a man for that.

"We hired him to work in our television broadcasts but I don't think he was ever comfortable with that. He just wasn't cut out to stand in front of a camera and interview people. He was a performer on the field, the best performer there was, but he wasn't a performer in the television studio. I'm surprised when I see him on television now with those commercials. He looks like he enjoys it; he does a good job and he seems very comfortable at it.

"It's amazing how he has held on to the public esteem. He is just a wonderful man, very warm and friendly now, and people just worship him wherever he goes. He knows how to deal with them now—never turns anybody away. He's just a nice man.

"He's a pretty good golfer, not a hack like me. He is very competitive on the golf course and he likes to win when he plays. It isn't like winning a game or winning a pennant, but he still likes to come out on top and gets a little miffed if he blows a short putt. He gets a little angry at himself when he does that but he gets over it in a hurry. The important thing is to get out there and have a good time and he's always doing that. We've been together at a few of those charity banquets at Vegas or in Los Angeles or a few other places and he has also become a very good speaker. Joe didn't like getting up and talking before a crowd, but he has gained experience and confidence in himself that way now and has developed into a very fine talker. He can tell a good story and he doesn't mind poking a little fun at himself if the situation calls for it.

"We had some great clubs and Joe DiMaggio was the best there was, on the field and off the field. It was always a kick to watch him play ball."

Tom DiMaggio was rushed now and he couldn't spend any more time. He stood up and started downstairs to his office. Just one thing more, he was asked. In 1951, when

170

Joe retired, many people said he could have played a year or two more. Many of his friends and his teammates say he was still a pretty good baseball player. Topping and Webb would have paid him a hundred thousand dollars again. Why did he quit?

Tom DiMaggio turned, walking slowly again toward his office. Then he stopped and looked back.

"Why did he quit? He quit because he wasn't Joe DiMaggio any more."

17: Miss Monroe

Retirement came easily to Joe DiMaggio in the spring of 1952. He spent his mornings in the restaurant near his San Francisco home, where he signed autographs for customers, drank coffee slowly, and read the sports pages. He dined with friends, played gin rummy at his club, watched television and made plans for returning East, when the baseball season began, to do a Yankee pregame and postgame show. Life was pleasant. The Yankees went off to train at St. Petersburg; he did not miss going. The Chicago White Sox trained at Pasadena; he was not down to watch. Invited to play golf with his good friend Lefty O'Doul, he played poorly his first time, stayed away from the course for two weeks, and took private lessons; the next time they played, he surprised O'Doul with long, straight drives.

One of the most written-about people in baseball in March 1952 was a husky slugger with the Philadelphia Athletics named Gus Zernial. A muscular home-run hitter, called Ozark Ike for his power and frame, Zernial was touted by sportswriters as the next DiMaggio. He had led the American League with thirty-three home runs the previous year. He was handsome, broad-shouldered, and on the verge of fame. David March, a Hollywood agent, called the Athletics and arranged for publicity pictures of the young ballplayer with his own new star client, a young actress who had been lifted to instant celebrity by her appearance in a nude centerfold in a new men's magazine. Her name was Marilyn Monroe.

Gus Zernial at fifty-one is still a handsome man. He works as a sportscaster with a CBS affiliate in Fresno, California. He remembered clearly how he led DiMaggio to Monroe.

"In the middle of spring training in 1952 I was told by the club to report to the park about an hour and a half before the scheduled start of the workout. There was a pretty girl that wanted to pose for some pictures with me. I was never against that, so I got there on time. The girl was making a movie and had also gotten a lot of publicity from the recent calendar shot in *Playboy*. I knew who she was.

"She was the most beautiful girl I had ever seen. Not only was she lovely, she was very intelligent. She wasn't a dumb blond. I talked to her for about two hours that day while they prepared all the cameras, and after the shooting. She hung around until after the workout began. I was tempted to ask her out for dinner that night but my wife was sitting in the stands.

"She was wearing shorts and a halter. It was a fantastic outfit. She was incredibly beautiful. We posed for pictures for about half an hour. She was squatting and I was told to wrap my arms around her and show her how to hold the bat. That was no problem. I enjoyed my work that day.

"The picture ran in all the papers. A few days later DiMaggio played in an exhibition game against us—I think it was a charity game—with a team made up of retired California players. He kidded me about the picture. 'How come I never get to pose with beautiful girls like that?' I told him this guy David March had arranged it. I guess he called March after that.

"I was a guest on Joe's television show at Yankee Stadium a couple of times after he met her. I tried to bring up her name. She was pretty famous then and they were going together. I never did. Joe was such a dignified guy. It just didn't seem right to ask him how he was doing with Marilyn."

Several days after Zernial posed with Marilyn, David March phoned her and persuaded her to go to dinner with DiMaggio, along with March and his date, at the Villa Nova Restaurant in Hollywood.

The time was set for seven o'clock. March and his friend were on time, and DiMaggio arrived fifteen minutes later. Marilyn did not arrive until nearly nine o'clock. DiMaggio stood up when she arrived, put out his hand, uttered a quiet hello, and sat down. According to published accounts of the evening, it was awkward for all four of them. DiMaggio was poor at small talk, and Marilyn addressed most of her conversation to March, talking about her picture *Monkey Business*. DiMaggio—dressed in a proper blue pinstriped suit, white shirt, and black shoes—sat straight-backed most of the evening.

Joe finally showed some animation when Mickey Rooney, dining in the same restaurant, spotted DiMaggio and the blond star and, uninvited, joined the party. A fanatic baseball fan, he spoke only to DiMaggio and began reciting all sorts of baseball feats Joe had performed. He recalled the series in Boston, a famous World Series home run, several other big hitting and fielding plays, the details of the famous 1941 streak. Marilyn, who had pretended to March that she had never heard of Joe DiMaggio, seemed impressed that Rooney would be so caught up in DiMaggio's mystique.

Shortly before eleven o'clock Marilyn said she had to be leaving; she had an early call the next day and had to get to sleep. DiMaggio had come to the restaurant by cab.

"Would you like me to drive you home?" Marilyn asked Joe.

"That would be very kind of you."

Marilyn and Joe left together and drove toward his hotel.

"I'm sorry I don't know anything about baseball," said Marilyn.

"That's all right," Joe replied. "I don't know much about movies."

She parked the car in front of his hotel. DiMaggio asked her if she would like to come up to his suite and look at some of his baseball trophies. Marilyn froze. She wasn't quite sure, she told an interviewer years later, whether DiMaggio was kidding or not. She repeated that she had to get up early the next morning. DiMaggio leaned over and softly kissed her. Marilyn pushed him away and said good night. DiMaggio said he would call her again. Marilyn did not answer. She drove home to her hotel.

March called late the next afternoon. "How'd you like him?" he asked.

"He struck out." She laughed. Marilyn obviously knew more about baseball than she had let on.

That night the phone rang. Marilyn was reading the script for the next day's shooting of *Monkey Business*. She answered the phone sleepily.

"This is Joe. Would you like to go out to dinner with me tomorrow night?"

"No. Thank you very much for asking. I'm busy."

"How about the next night?"

"No, I'm busy then too. Call me some other time."

She said good-by and hung up. DiMaggio called her the next day and asked again. She refused. He called the following afternoon. She refused again. He called every evening for two weeks and she refused every time. She gave him no encouragement at all. Finally he stopped calling. A week went by. The phone rang in DiMaggio's suite. It was Marilyn.

"Would you like to take me to dinner tonight?" she asked.

They began dating regularly. She trusted DiMaggio. He was honest, sincere, and solid. He made her feel loved and protected. He gave her strength and she understood his silences.

The romance became public, and the studio made the most of it. Joe accompanied Marilyn to the set as she worked. Their names filled the gossip columns. He dined with her in the best-known restaurants in Hollywood, and in San Francisco and New York. He called her every day from wherever he was. There were rumors of impending marriage. Both denied them.

"We're just friends," DiMaggio told reporters, in classic rejoinder.

DiMaggio had a strange pull on Marilyn. He was the father she never knew—the strong, silent man who encouraged her. He seemed to delight in her success. He had achieved fame in his own right so he hardly needed to use hers. She was comfortable with him. She could take off her shoes in his apartment; he could take off his jacket and tie in hers. They deposited clothes in each other's apartments. The attraction was strong and obvious.

The romance had its difficult moments. DiMaggio was jealous of any attention she showed other men. She reminded him gently that they were not married and pointed out that publicity was a vital part of her career. He raised his voice to her on several such occasions. Still, he was generally loving and kind.

One day they kidded about all the famous people they each knew and all the famous people they had posed with for pictures.

"I guess the most famous I have ever posed with," DiMaggio told her, "were Douglas MacArthur and Ethel Barrymore. You're prettier."

"My heart jumped when he said I was pretty," Marilyn told a friend. "Men had been saying that all my life. This was different. This wasn't a man saying that because he wanted something of me. This was a man who sincerely cared for me. He was saying something from his heart."

On Christmas Eve 1952 Marilyn went to a holiday party at the studio. She went alone; Joe was out of town. Christmas was an empty, unhappy season for Marilyn Monroe. There were no pleasant childhood memories. Her father had deserted the family; her mother was mentally ill. There had been a series of foster homes, unconcerned guardians. She had married at sixteen. Her young life had been one ache piled on another.

Marilyn left the party early and went back to her suite at the Beverly Hills Hotel. As she opened the door, she suddenly saw a small Christmas tree sitting on a table across the room. There was a card. She read it eagerly. It said, "Merry Christmas, Marilyn," and its was signed, "Joe." On the other side of the room was a man sitting in a chair—Joe.

"This is the first time in my life anyone has ever given me a Christmas tree," she said. "Joe, I love you." DiMaggio had ordered dinner. They got a little drunk on champagne and fell asleep in each other's arms.

The cross-country romance continued for another year. DiMaggio spent a great deal of time in San Francisco and New York. He saw her when he could. He constantly sent gifts. He bought her a ten-thousand-dollar mink coat.

DiMaggio began his career as a television broadcaster for the Yankees. When Marilyn could get to town, she would sit in the stands at Yankee Stadium or in the studio under the stands and watch him interview ballplayers.

"A lot of guys used to hang around that studio just to see her," Phil Rizzuto recalled. "She was really gorgeous. She'd sit in the stands before the games and talk to some of the players. They were kids and just liked the idea of going home and telling their friends they knew a movie star. They really liked and admired her.

"Joe used to bring her to Shor's a lot in those days. They had a special table and Toots would protect them. Joe's a very proud and dignified guy, and he didn't like all the men looking at her. Joe is a jealous guy. But I think there is one main point to remember about Joe and Marilyn. Joe loved her. I know that."

DiMaggio was unsure of himself in the TV interviews, but he was making fifty thousand dollars a year from the Yankees for the programs, so he forced himself to do them. The show was performed live in a small studio next to the Yankee clubhouse in the stadium. DiMaggio would interview the star of the game, asking routine questions and getting routine answers. He was mostly concerned with reading the cue cards correctly and getting the Ballantine Beer commercials in the right place.

Jackie Farrell, an ex-newspaperman who had worked for the Yanks for many years, was the nominal producer of the show. It was his job to present the guest to DiMaggio before and after each game, lead him through the maze of cue cards, cameras, and red lights, and handle any difficulties.

"I had Dizzy Dean and Joe E. Brown and Red Barber on that show. DiMaggio was the easiest guy to work with. He never gave me any problems. He was a great man, a great player, and he never changed at all when he went on television. I kept reminding him that he just had to be himself to be a success. He wasn't temperamental. He was very easy to handle. He was uncomfortable in front of the camera—there was no getting away from that—and a little insecure. About the only time I ever saw him get upset was when we were getting ready to do the show one day and we didn't have all the cue cards in place. There was one cue card we used every day for him to open the show. This one day it was misplaced and it was a few minutes before the opener. He got a little excited and said if we didn't get the card out there, he wasn't going to do the show. We finally found it and he went on without a fuss."

Joe's stage fright was obvious. The cue card that Farrell was looking for and finally found read, "Hi. I'm Joe Di-Maggio. Welcome to the Joe DiMaggio Show."

DiMaggio did not return to host the program in 1953 but became involved in a television show for children. He demonstrated batting and fielding techniques and found that a lot easier to do, having always gotten on well with kids.

Joe's fame remained steady, even after his retirement as an active player. Marilyn's continued to grow, due partly to relentless publicity, partly to some successful movies, and partly to her romance with DiMaggio.

The rumors persisted that DiMaggio and Monroe would marry. Both denied it, but they were seen together very frequently.

Marilyn seemed to find a charm and warmth in DiMaggio she had never found in any other man. He treated her gently and could kid her in a loving way.

She once mentioned to him that when she was a schoolgirl all her friends called her Stringbean.

"If they called you Stringbean, honey," DiMaggio said, "they must have been looking at you in a room with an awful low ceiling."

178

As happened so often in Marilyn's life, the pain of a professional setback triggered a deep personal reaction. Twentieth Century Fox had been battling with Marilyn for many months. She was demanding more money because of her new stardom. She also wanted certain conditions written into her contract and expressed her dislike of the types of films the studio selected for her. *Pink Tights,* a new movie with Frank Sinatra, she found beneath her. The studio suspended her in early January.

On January 14, 1954, early in the morning, Harry Brand, the veteran publicity head of Twentieth, received a breathless call from Marilyn.

"Harry, I'm being married to Joe this afternoon," she said.

Once she had promised Brand that he would be the first to know if she were to marry. She had kept her promise. Now she was ready to become Mrs. Joe DiMaggio.

At three o'clock in the afternoon Joe and Marilyn drove up to the San Francisco City Hall, slipped unnoticed through a side door, and walked quickly to the chamber of Municipal Court Judge Charles S. Perry. Arrangements had been completed only minutes before by DiMaggio's friend Reno Barsocchini. Reno and Lefty O'Doul and Lefty's wife, along with Marilyn, Joe, and the judge, were the only people in the room. Marilyn wore a chocolate-brown suit with a white ermine collar and carried a corsage of three white orchids. DiMaggio wore a blue suit and a blue polka-dot tie. The ceremony took five minutes.

The news had leaked, and more than a hundred reporters, photographers, and curious fans gathered in the corridors outside the judge's chambers. They closed in on the newlyweds as they emerged. Photographers again and again urged Marilyn to kiss Joe. She complied, and DiMaggio laughed and blushed. Reporters shouted questions. DiMaggio answered most.

"We decided to go through with it a few days ago," DiMaggio said. "It isn't a snap judgment, as you know. We have talked about it for some time."

"We are both very happy," Marilyn said in that wispy voice of hers.

They started edging away, trying to get through the crowd.

"How many kids do you want?" someone asked.

"I'd like to have six," said Marilyn.

"At least one," said DiMaggio.

"Where you gonna live?"

"Here, San Francisco," DiMaggio replied.

"I'm going to continue my career," added Marilyn, "but I'm looking forward to being a housewife too."

They pushed through the throng, made their way down the stairs, got into their car with help from several policemen, waved, and drove off. They raced out of the city to shake several pursuing photographers, DiMaggio driving his blue Cadillac with the Joe D license plates. Three hours later they pulled off the road at the Clifton Motel in the tiny beach town of Paso Robles. Proprietor Ernest Sharpe, according to his later recollection, was watching television as the office door of his motel opened. He looked up and Joe DiMaggio was staring at him.

"Well, I'll be," said Sharpe.

"Hi. We'd like a room."

"I don't suppose you'd want twin beds," he said.

"No," said DiMaggio. "We'd like a double bed and a room with a television set."

"I've got just the thing for you," Sharpe said. "Number fifteen."

He volunteered to help DiMaggio with his bags, was introduced to the bride, asked if there was anything else, and left the honeymoon couple alone.

Sharpe went back into the office and phoned his wife. "You won't believe who just pulled in here and rented room fifteen," he said. "Joe DiMaggio and Marilyn Monroe."

"You're right, Ernest," said Mrs. Sharpe. "I won't believe it."

Fifteen hours later DiMaggio came back into the office, settled the bill, signed an autograph for Sharpe, and drove off with Marilyn to a Mexican honeymoon.

While they were in Mexico, the results of the 1954 Hall of Fame voting were made known. Rabbit Maranville, Bill Dickey, and Bill Terry were admitted to the Hall of Fame. DiMaggio had received 175 votes by sportswriters across the country. He needed 189. That he had not been elected was not remarkable. Very few players had ever made it the first time they were eligible. A year later, on January 26, 1955, DiMaggio was elected as a member of Baseball's Hall of Fame.

Lefty O'Doul had gotten DiMaggio to agree to play several exhibition games in Japan early in 1954. Joe decided to extend his honeymoon and take Marilyn with him. He had been there several times and was considered almost as famous a personality in Japan as he was in the United States. Marilyn and Joe flew out of San Francisco late in January and checked into the Imperial Hotel in Tokyo. The Korean War had just recently ended, but more than a million GIs still remained in Korea. Marilyn received a request from the United States government to fly to Seoul and entertain the troops. DiMaggio was against the trip but could not keep her from going. Marilyn felt it important. She went to Korea, entertained more than a hundred thousand cheering soldiers at a huge airport show, and was thrilled as pictures of her were flashed around the world. Joe was sullen when she returned.

"Joe, Joe," she exclaimed, "you've never heard such cheering!"

"Yes, I have," Joe said quietly.

When they returned to America, Marilyn was to go to

work on her new movie, *The Seven Year Itch*. They rented a mansion in Beverly Hills, and it became a tourist attraction. Once their address was known, they couldn't relax at home. They couldn't dine in a public restaurant. Their every move was reported to the papers. Their marriage was played out in the nation's press.

The film Marilyn was working on was going badly, and often she came home exhausted. She was having trouble sleeping and was taking pills. The phone never stopped ringing, and Hollywood types appeared on their doorstep at all hours.

DiMaggio flew off to New York to attend some business, and Marilyn followed when the shooting of her movie moved there. The pace continued. DiMaggio became more withdrawn. He spent long hours at Shor's. Marilyn went with him occasionally but felt as uncomfortable there, among the sporting crowd and cigar smoke, as DiMaggio had among the Hollywood set.

Jimmy Cannon, one of DiMaggio's few intimates, wrote a column in the New York *Post* about the couple's life together.

"She likes what I like," DiMaggio told Cannon. "She's a quiet girl. My life is dull. I never interfere with Marilyn's work. She goes to the studio and I don't go with her any more. It's the same stuff all the time. They do a scene and then they hang around a long time waiting to look at it. I don't resent her fame. She was working long before she met me. And for what? What has she got after all these years? She works like a dog. When she's working, she's up at five or six in the morning and doesn't get through until seven at night. We eat dinner, watch a little television, and go to bed."

Arthur Richman, director of promotion for the New York Mets, stared at a picture on his office wall at Shea Stadium. It was of himself and a smiling DiMaggio.

"I don't know if Joe will talk to me after this. It's just one thing he doesn't want discussed. It's the quickest way to lose him as a friend, to talk about Marilyn. He still has tremendous love and feeling for her. There was a night I was with him in Los Angeles. He just started talking about her. He mentioned something about Beverly Hills and how they had this beautiful house there. He said the house was like Grand Central Station. There was no privacy. The phones never stopped ringing. It seemed everybody could get their number. People could ring the bell and knock on the door at all hours. It didn't matter if it were three o'clock in the morning or three o'clock in the afternoon, people kept coming to the front door. Joe thought maybe part of the problem was living in Los Angeles. He wanted her to move to San Francisco with him. He told me he asked her to give up her career and live quietly with him as his wife. He asked her to think about it shortly after they were married. She said she would. He told her she didn't have to decide that minute. She could think about it and make her own decision. Joe said the marriage seemed to go wrong from their honeymoon in Japan on. They had gone there together on a beautiful trip after they were married. The Defense Department found out Marilyn and Joe were honeymooning in Japan. They sent over some general to ask her if she would go to Korea and entertain the troops. Joe said, 'Marilyn looked at me and I looked at her. I told her to go ahead if she wanted to.' Marilyn went and Joe stayed back alone in Japan on his honeymoon. That was a hell of a way to start a marriage."

When Marilyn was filming *The Seven Year Itch,* one scene required her to stand over a subway grating with the wind lifting her skirt. Photographers recorded the memorable sight. Onlookers cheered. DiMaggio was standing off to the side watching the scene and was disgusted. He could not separate the fact that the actress performing the rituals demanded of her profession was also his wife. He turned sharply and walked away. He went to Shor's and drank heavily that night. He was bitter about the photo in the next day's newspapers. It helped make Marilyn an even bigger star—the shaky film became a smash—but helped destroy the marriage.

DiMaggio flew back to San Francisco the next day. Several days later Marilyn returned to Los Angeles and DiMaggio joined her in their Beverly Hills home.

In another part of the country, Joe Page was suddenly arrested on a complaint filed by his wife and charged with desertion and nonsupport. Unable to post bond, he spent the night in a cell.

There was a phone call the next day, a quick telegram, a mysterious cabling of money for his bail. Officials had no idea where the funds came from. The money was simply brought to court by a local lawyer and Page was free. He had not seen DiMaggio for four years, but baseball people said Joe had been responsible for bailing Page out, though neither Page nor DiMaggio would ever comment on the ex-pitcher's night in the jailhouse.

On October 5, 1954, just 274 days after they were married, Marilyn Monroe, using her legal name of Norma Jeane DiMaggio, as plaintiff, requested a divorce from Joseph Paul DiMaggio, defendant, in the Superior Court of the state of California.

Marilyn had cried most of the night before and had been under sedation. Her attorney, Jerry Giesler, who represented all sorts of Hollywood stars, had talked with Marilyn in the bedroom of her home while Joe remained downstairs. Marilyn had signed the divorce-decree request but declined to appear in court. The next day Giesler exhibited the decree request to the press.

The divorce complaint charged that DiMaggio had caused

her "grievous mental suffering and anguish." The complaint said there was no community property, and Marilyn did not seek any alimony.

For several days the columnists studied the breakup of the king of baseball and the queen of the movies. There were reports that DiMaggio had been upset by the attention Marilyn paid to her voice coach. "There is no other man," Marilyn told columnist Sidney Skolsky. "There never has been."

DiMaggio quickly agreed that the breakup had not been caused by any other party. "I want to be a good friend to Marilyn. I have nothing else to say except 'no comment.' If she wants the divorce, she will get it."

18: Carrying the Torch

Jerry Coleman saw DiMaggio soon after the breakup.

"I remember when he split with Marilyn. We all talked about it among ourselves but nobody ever brought it up with him. Nobody ever brought up anything personal with Joe. I have never mentioned Marilyn's name to him and he has never mentioned it to me. But I'm sure of one thing. Joe DiMaggio deeply loved that woman. They had split but he still was carrying the torch. Everybody who knew him agreed to that."

Joe DiMaggio retreated from public view for a long time after the divorce. He stayed mainly in San Francisco. He played golf with Lefty O'Doul, dined often with Reno Barsocchini. Once or twice a year he returned East—to participate in the Yankees' Old Timers' Day, to make a charity appearance, to play golf at the Westchester Country Club. He would see old friends: George Solotaire, Jimmy Cannon, and a few others. Almost always, when he visited the East, he would fly to Washington and spend time with Edward Bennett Williams, the well-known Washington attorney.

Edward Bennett Williams, in the course of his amazing career, has represented such clients as mobster Frank Costello, newscaster David Brinkley, football coach Vince Lombardi, Yankee baseball owner George Steinbrenner III, and the Washington *Post*. Williams also represents the Democratic National Committee, is considered a power in Democratic politics, and filed the Democratic party's civil suit against the Committee to Reelect the President shortly after the Watergate burglary. Strongly interested in sports, he bought into and became president of the Washington Redskins football team. He has been a friend of Joe DiMaggio's, and his attorney, for twenty-five years.

"I talk to Joe a great deal on the phone. He calls me from San Francisco or I call him from Washington. When Norman Mailer's book on Marilyn came out, he called me immediately. He was very hurt. 'What can we do about it?' I told him, 'Joe, just sit tight and don't discuss it. There isn't anything we can do. You'll only help him more by making a fuss about it.' He had gotten some obscene mail after the book came out. He was very hurt. He was hurt by a lot of things Mailer said in the book about Marilyn.

"Joe carries a torch bigger than the Statue of Liberty. It has not lessened through the years. He was crazy about her. Still is. It has not diminished. He has deep feelings about the whole Hollywood crowd, about the people who abused her. He has not gotten over certain things and probably never will.

"I used to come to New York on business when he was still playing for the Yankees and I would eat at Toots' place. I met Joe there and we became friends. Those were the days at the end of his career, 1950 and 1951, when he was suffering so badly with different injuries and ailments. He had that one throw in his arm and then he couldn't lift it. There were times his arm was hurting so badly after a game that Joe Page would have to comb his hair.

"I went out with Joe to a fight the first night he returned to Yankee Stadium after he retired as a player. It was a great night. It was the Robinson-Basilio fight, one of the greatest ever. We had dinner at Shor's and then we all went up to the fight together—me, Joe, Toots, Averell Harriman, Marie Harriman, and Ernest Hemingway and Mary.

"We walked up the ramp toward our seats and the kids spotted him and started going crazy. There was applause and shouting and everyone was yelling his name. 'Joe, Joe, Joe D.' They surrounded him with their autograph pads and the crowd was so thick we couldn't move to our seats. Joe was very happy that night, being back and being remembered, and he was signing all the autographs. The crowd around him was enormous. Finally an usher came over, saw that it was DiMaggio, and started to pull the kids away so we could get to our seats. One kid gets Joe's autograph and starts walking back to his seat to show it to his friends. He looks up and he sees Papa Hemingway off to the side. Nobody had recognized him. They had all fussed over DiMaggio. This one kid stared at Papa's beard for a minute, looked up at him, and said, 'Hey, you're somebody, ain'tcha?' Papa never blinked. 'Yeah, I'm his doctor.'

"We used to go to a lot of fights together. Joe really loved the big fights. I used to stay at the Madison Hotel in New York when I came in, and Joe stayed there a lot too. We used to eat at Shor's or at an Italian place he liked called Joe and Rose's and then go over to the Harwyn Club. That was one of the hot nightspots in those days. Nobody had the kind of instant identification Joe had. In all my years in Washington and New York, only two people have had that in any public place I've been in. Joe is one.

David Brinkley is the other. I don't think anybody else is in their class.

"Joe loves football. I bought the Redskins in 1965 and Joe and I met all over the country at Redskin games. I have a lot of kids, seven of them, from age nineteen to age eight, and they are all crazy about him. Every time I go to a Redskin game out of town, I take one of my kids and I let the kid take a friend. If it's a game that Joe is coming to, they just talk about Joe all week. Once they see him they forget all about the football game. The amazing thing about Joe's fame is that it carries over to young people, like my own kids, who were not even born when he last played. He just has an incredible hold on people.

"Joe is probably the most self-effacing man I have ever met. It is impossible to get him to talk about himself. We go to these games and the fans stand up and cheer him and Joe sort of hides. He doesn't think it's right to stand up and take a bow or wave to a crowd in a ball park. He wants to be left alone, to be treated like another fan. He seems to find it impossible to realize he isn't another fan. Hell, he's Joe DiMaggio.

"A couple of years ago Joe stayed with us over Christmas. That's always a tough time of the year for him. We were playing the San Francisco 49ers and he agreed to stay with us so he could see the game. We gave him some gifts and he gave us some gifts and the kids all gave him gifts and he really enjoyed himself. He probably felt he was imposing but that was ridiculous. I invited him the next Christmas but he wouldn't come. Joe is a very lonely man at times. I think Christmas is about the worst time for him. He usually goes off by himself to Vegas and plays golf out there. He likes to fish and I know that he has taken off in his boat around Christmas a few times so he wouldn't bother anybody and nobody would bother him.

"I've represented him in most of his business deals

188

through the years. We handled the business dealings for his bank commercial. That brings him a lot of money and has given him a great deal of security. Now he has that coffee commercial and that's been very successful for him. Joe doesn't like binding commitments in any business deals. He won't take anything that locks him up for a long period of time. He likes to be able to go off some place when he feels like it. Joe doesn't like to work too much. That's just one of the facts of life about him.

"I don't think Joe has squandered his money through the years. I wouldn't say he is a very wealthy man but I'm certain he has made enough to live very comfortably. Most of these business deals he makes bring him a good deal of money without having to work very hard for it. I think Joe likes to enjoy his retirement without too much pressure and work. He worked hard and felt the pressure every day of his professional baseball life. Now he has time for relaxation and he intends to enjoy it. Joe DiMaggio would never get into a deal simply because he could make a lot of money at it. That's not his style. He doesn't care that much about accumulating money and he really doesn't need a fortune. He lives well, does what he wants, travels where he wants, enjoys himself, and has enough for all of that.

"Joe is a good friend and will do you a favor any time you ask. An example was when I got involved in the Wong Sun case. It's a landmark decision in constitutional law. Wong Sun was a Chinese laundryman with a small shop in San Francisco. Every kid in law school knows the case. I was retained after the Supreme Court agreed to hear it.

"There were many unanswered questions. The main legal question was whether or not the police had a reasonable basis for going to this particular laundry. It had merely been described as a laundry on Leavenworth Street. The record didn't show how many there were. That would be the deciding point.

"I was working late at night in my office. I decided that I wanted to remind the Supreme Court the next day of this very point. I picked up the phone and called Joe DiMaggio at home and got him out of bed. 'Joe, you have to do something for me right now. Go out and count the Chinese laundries on Leavenworth Street.' Joe didn't hesitate a minute. He didn't ask my why. He just knew that if I was calling him at this hour with that kind of strange request he would do it immediately. He knew it was important. He got dressed and went down to Leavenworth Street and started counting the laundries.

"I was with Joe when Arthur Miller was called to testify before the House Un-American Activities Committee. Joe and Marilyn had been divorced but, of course, Joe was still carrying the torch. Marilyn had married Miller and Joe was upset. Marilyn volunteered to testify for Miller at the hearings. She got up before the committee, defended Miller vigorously, and said, 'Arthur Miller is the only man I ever loved.' I knew that would hit Joe like a brick wall. I figured he would cancel our dinner date that evening. He didn't. He went straight ahead with it and never said a word about Marilyn all night. Joe has a way of blocking unpleasant things out of his mind like that. If he doesn't want to discuss something that would hurt him, he just forgets about it.

"Every once in a while, not very often, Joe gets into a mood where he likes to reminisce. If you push him about telling stories of his playing days, he usually won't do it. If you don't, it might come up accidentally and he'll talk about it. This one time we were talking about our football team and how George Allen motivates them and how motivation is such an important part of the success of a professional athlete. Joe just started talking about his playing days. 'When I was playing ball, there would be sixty thousand people in Yankee Stadium and I would burn inside because

190

I wanted to hit the ball so badly. I wanted to be the greatest I could be. I burned in my belly to be the best there was.'

"As he told the story, you could see his eyes flash back to those days and you could almost see him going after a ball or getting a big hit or stealing a base. He put pressures on himself as a player that were beyond belief. He wanted to be the greatest ever, and there was no settling for anything else.

"Joe went on. 'We would get on a train after playing before all those people in the stadium, and we would ride all night to St. Louis. Joe Page wanted to go out as soon as we got there and have a few drinks or chase some girls and I didn't want to do it because I felt I had to be ready the next day. There might be a kid in the stands, or five kids or ten, who had never seen me play or would never see me play again. I burned to be the best there was for them, to leave them with a good memory of me.'

"Joe always felt that he had an obligation to himself and to the ball club and to the fans—even if there were only six hundred in the stands in St. Louis—to play the very best he knew how every single day. His commitment to himself was incredible. He could never take the pressure off himself. I have only met one other man in my life that had that kind of incredible pride and determination and was so hard on himself. That was Vince Lombardi. We had him with us in 1969, and Joe and Vince got to be very good friends. They really understood each other. I think they knew each other well from New York, but when Vince coached for us they became much closer friends.

"Vince and I had been on a trip to Vietnam and we came back through San Francisco. We called Joe and had dinner with him at this out-of-the-way place in San Jose. It was one of the great all-time nights. The guy that ran the place almost went nuts when he found out he had Joe DiMaggio and Vince Lombardi in his place at the same time. We had

191

a marvelous evening and Joe and Vince really got along beautifully. There was a fantastic rapport. It was as if they had each dedicated their lives to excellence and understood each other in a way few people ever understand someone else.

"There have been a couple of times through the years when Joe talked about getting back into baseball. It was his first love and he felt a little bitter that there wasn't a place for him in the game. The Yankees kept making vague promises about jobs but nothing ever seemed to come of it. I don't know if it was the fault of the Yankees or partly Joe's own fault. There were things that he simply didn't want to be pinned down on, and I think a permanent job with the Yankees was one of them.

"Finally, a few years ago—1968, I think it was—Joe got a call from Charlie Finley. He was moving his Kansas City ball club to Oakland and he wanted Joe to work for him. Finley thought Joe would be a good influence on the public and would help give the A's a very important identification through Joe with the San Francisco Bay area. That was a vital part of Finley's plan in moving out there. Finley spoke to Joe and explained the deal. Joe was interested. He wouldn't have to move away from his San Francisco home and he would be working on his own terms and at his own pace.

"Finley knew what he wanted and was easy to work with. We got together on a deal, and Joe went back to baseball with the Oakland club. He was really happy doing that.

"I think Joe enjoyed the job very much. The young players were very friendly to him and enjoyed having him there for advice. When the A's won the pennant, Joe was very proud. A lot of those same players were the players he helped when he was with the A's. Reggie Jackson was one of his pet projects. He knew Jackson had enormous ability. It was simply a question of bringing it out.

"Joe stayed with Finley for two years and then he got tired of being tied down again. A lot of people who hadn't seen him for a while realized he was back in the game and he got some feelers about managing. That was one thing he said he would never do. He just wouldn't enjoy the responsibility and he wouldn't want to travel as much as ball clubs have to travel nowadays.

"I enjoyed it very much when Joe was with the A's because he used to come into Washington regularly—we had a baseball team here then—and we would go out to dinner and have a grand time. My kids always worshipped him and they got a great kick out of seeing him in his Oakland uniform.

"Joe has a marvelous way with kids. He seems to loosen up and really relax when he is around kids. I guess he really doesn't want people using him or taking advantage of him, and he knows that kids only care for him for himself. I see him give a kid an autograph in a ball park sometimes and I realize it's almost as much fun for Joe to be giving the autograph as it is for the kid to be getting it.

"Now that Joe isn't with the A's and we don't have a team in Washington, I have to call him at his house in San Francisco when I'm trying to get him. His sister Marie runs the house and she always knows where he is. I call her and she tells me he's in Vegas or Los Angeles or New York or some place. Joe's a hard guy to find. If I want to get him to a game on Sunday, I have to start calling him on the Monday before to make sure we make connections.

"After all these years he still looks about the same as when I first met him. I don't think he has put on five pounds in twenty years. He is very careful about what he eats and watches himself all the time. If he knows he is going out for dinner he usually doesn't have anything all day but tea.

"Joe is also far better-looking today than he was as a young man. He dresses beautifully and everything is just right, and he has that tall, slim appearance that makes all clothes look good on him. I know all the women find him extremely attractive.

"I guess Joe is a relatively happy man these days. He has many, many friends all over the country and he plays in all these golf tournaments and he is so easily recognized that everybody fusses over him and makes things easy for him. He likes to fish a lot now and he does a great deal of fishing when he is home in San Francisco. I guess that's one of the reasons he stays out there. The climate is great and he can play golf or fish every day of the year. He couldn't do that if he lived in Washington or New York.

"Next week I'll be seeing Joe in New York at the cerebral palsy charity dinner. That's the kind of place I catch him at most these days."

19: Farewell to Marilyn

They had been man and wife once, and now they were friends. It seemed a warmer, more solid, more pleasing relationship than the one they had had as a married couple.

In public she called him Mr. D, and he always called her Miss Monroe. They were on the phone to each other frequently, dined together on occasion, shared a birthday party or a holiday, talked often of Joe's son. Marilyn was fond of Joe Junior.

"I can't take the place of your mother because you have a mother," Marilyn had told the thirteen-year-old boy when she married his father, "but I'd like to be your friend." Young Joe called her often through the years, visited her, and leaned on her as he would an older sister. They remained close through his late teens and early twenties, despite the disapproval of his mother.

DiMaggio seemed always on the periphery of Marilyn Monroe's life through the 1950s, even after her marriage to playwright Arthur Miller in 1956. By 1960, as Marilyn worked on Miller's film *The Misfits,* the marriage was in decline. She found the filming difficult and there were hysterics, subtle threats of suicide, pills, alcohol. Early in 1961 there was a divorce from Miller and more turmoil, more pills, less sleep, more contact with DiMaggio. In February she collapsed in her New York apartment on Sutton Place and in March was taken to the Payne-Whitney Clinic, a fashionable establishment for people suffering mental disorders. She hated Payne-Whitney and wanted to leave. She phoned DiMaggio at St. Petersburg Beach where he was working with the Yankees, and he caught the next plane to New York. He rushed to the clinic, arranged for Marilyn's transfer to Columbia Presbyterian Hospital, and persuaded her, after a time, to come to Florida.

There they went fishing together and relaxed on the beach. Joe brought her to Yankee training camp occasionally, and the young players were thrilled.

At the end of spring training, Joe and Marilyn stayed in Florida for several more days. Then Joe took her back to Los Angeles. She was to make a new movie with Dean Martin called *Something's Got to Give.* Joe returned to his San Francisco home and phoned her almost daily.

Marilyn had been accepted into the fringes of the Hollywood Rat Pack, with Dean Martin, Sammy Davis, Jr., Joey Bishop, Peter Lawford, and packmaster Frank Sinatra, and was often seen with them in Hollywood and Las Vegas. Hints of an affair with Sinatra were dismissed as studio gossip.

In June Marilyn was fired from the production of *Some-*

195

thing's Got to Give and the picture was suspended. She retreated to her new home in Brentwood, drank heavily, and
took pills indiscriminately. She was out of work and lonely.

DiMaggio's life had been calm through the late 1950s.
Golf had become his passion. There were friends in San
Francisco to play with, and business associates and new
acquaintances at every club he was invited to. He was also
occupied by the first serious job outside baseball he ever
held, a one-hundred-thousand-dollar-a-year position as a
representative of the V. H. Monette Company of Smithfield,
Virginia.

The owner of the company, Valmore Monette, was a
friend of Sid Luckman's, the former Chicago Bears quarterback, who in turn was a friend of DiMaggio's. The company was the main supplier for post exchanges on American
military bases around the world. In 1958, on the recom-
mendation of Luckman, Monette hired Joe DiMaggio.

"It worked out beautifully. Joe and I used to travel together around the world. We would visit these different
Army bases, and Joe would get involved with the kids and
give baseball exhibitions. All these bases have Little League
teams with the sons of the military, and Joe would talk to
them, demonstrate things for them, sign autographs, and
help them. They loved him. Everybody did. We would play
a little golf with the commanding officers of the base, talk
a little baseball and a little business, and have a grand old
time.

"I guess we traveled everywhere when Joe was with us.
We were in Europe a great deal—Germany, Italy, France,
places like that—and visited some of the bases in the Far
East and most here in the United States. We kept Joe busy.
It was quite a schedule and he did a terrific job for us.

"He was just a fine person. You know why he left us?
Nobody knows this. I never told anybody before. I didn't

think it was right. Now it seems okay because so many years have passed. Joe left us on August 1, 1962, because he was flying back to California to ask Marilyn to marry him again. He told me he had talked to Marilyn and thought she had finally agreed to leave the movies and remarry him and move with him to San Francisco. He loved her a great deal and they had always been in contact, and he told me that he had decided to remarry her. He thought things would be different than they had been before and that everything would work out well for them now. I was shocked when I heard what happened to Marilyn because I knew that was why he was going back out there in 1962."

DiMaggio quit his job with Monette some four days before Marilyn's death and flew to San Francisco to play in an exhibition game on Saturday, August 4. He apparently planned to fly down to Los Angeles on August 5 to see Marilyn. But when he arrived in Los Angeles that day it was to arrange for her burial.

On the morning after her death DiMaggio took charge of the funeral arrangements. He decided she would be buried with dignity, free of the hysterical commotion usually associated with rites for Hollywood idols. He limited the funeral attendance to twenty-three close friends—non-Hollywood. He chose the Village Church of Westwood for the service and Westwood Memorial Park for the burial. No press was to be allowed inside the small chapel.

At the funeral the face of DiMaggio was that of a tortured man. His son, in the dress uniform of a Marine private, was red-eyed and erect. When an uninvited person —Marilyn's attorney, Milton Rudin—tried to enter the chapel, DiMaggio at first was adamant.

"You are keeping out Marilyn's close friends," Rudin protested.

"If it hadn't been for some of her friends," DiMaggio

replied, "she wouldn't be where she is." But he allowed Rudin to come in. Others he denied.

Patricia Lawford, sister of President John F. Kennedy, had flown from Hyannisport for the funeral. She was excluded. So were Peter Lawford, Frank Sinatra, Dean Martin, and Gene Kelly.

The service was short. When it was over, DiMaggio stood at the chapel door and shook hands with the guests, thanking each for coming. A helicopter whirled overhead, shooting crowd scenes.

Lois Weber Smith was with Marilyn Monroe from 1955 to 1960 as her press agent.

"I don't think Joe was right with what he did with the funeral, but I know that she cared very deeply for him in the last years. He was a solid guy, very dependable, very helpful to her. For a while, when they were married, Marilyn had the idea she could have both lives, the private and the public. She deceived herself in that. She couldn't keep them separate. The press wouldn't allow it. They were both too big, too famous, too much a part of America to just disappear when they weren't working.

"I know he loved her. I'm convinced of that now. I know in her way she loved him too. He was kind and generous with her and strong. It was almost as if Marilyn Monroe and Joe DiMaggio met at the wrong time in their lives.

"I remember once when Marilyn phoned me—it was probably in the middle of 1955. She was staying at the Waldorf Towers and called me about some publicity we had scheduled. I could hear this pounding noise over the phone as she talked very calmly. She didn't refer to the noise for a while, but she could soon tell by my voice that it puzzled me. Finally she said, 'Oh, that's Joe banging on the door outside.' She continued the conversation for several minutes with that noise still going on before she hung up.

"My attitude then was that I didn't like Joe, from what Marilyn told me about him. I never met him or saw them together. I don't know whether what she told me was for effect or not. I couldn't always be certain she wasn't playing some role. I am sure Marilyn was afraid of him, physically afraid. She said Joe had a bad temper. He was obviously rigid in his beliefs. There must have been a great ambivalence in his feelings toward her. He wanted her for all the reasons any other man would want her, because she was a gorgeous woman, but didn't want her to be like that for any other man. It was an impossibility.

"Later I realized through the years that the attraction remained great. Marilyn knew where she stood with Joe. There was great relief in that for her, a woman whose life was so unsettled. He was always there; she could always call on him. Joe never asked anything of her. She could lean on him, depend on him, be certain of him. It was a marvelous feeling of comfort for her.

"She spoke often of Joe's son. She cared for him a great deal. There was a big part of Marilyn that yearned for that 'normal life.' She loved children; she loved animals. She desperately wanted children of her own. She was marvelous with children, very warm, very friendly, very affectionate, completely without guile. She would put herself out for children. She was close to Arthur Miller's. She said to them, 'I want to be your friend.' She had a beautiful honesty with children. There was a part of her that obviously wanted to be part of Joe's family, the brothers and the sisters, the big spaghetti dinners, the warmth and the happiness of a large Italian family. I think she really would have liked to be part of Joe's family that way, sort of adopting them as her family, as the family she never had.

"Marilyn loved people; she loved life. Her moods could be mercurial but she could be so terribly enthusiastic about a project. There were times she talked of Joe with great

199

warmth. There were times she made it clear he had hurt her very badly, maybe even struck her, in some jealous rage. I am certain Joe loved her very deeply. He was a jealous man and couldn't accept her as a love object for every other man in the world.

"I believe Joe made a mistake at the end, I mean that utter rejection of everybody in the movie industry at the funeral. That was not fair of him. They were important to her. They were helpful to her; she chose that industry and many of those people. It was not right to keep them away. She would have wanted a Hollywood funeral. I imagine he thought he could restore some purity to her that way, to bury her with the calm and dignity he had wished for them in their lives."

The office of Westwood Village Mortuary at Memorial Park is run by Angelo DeLucia. It is indeed true, he said, that DiMaggio has arranged to have flowers at Marilyn's grave continually. "Three times a week a truck pulls up here from the Parisian Florist in Westwood. The driver gets out and puts six red roses in a small vase next to Marilyn's crypt. Rain or shine those flowers are delivered."

"C'mon," said DeLucia. "I'll show you where it is."

He walked out of his office. Just across from the office, on a small piece of the green, are some footstones. DeLucia stopped. "Look at this one. That was Marilyn's aunt. She was buried here and Marilyn came here often to see it. I don't know that much about it but I've been told she was very close to that aunt. The reason Marilyn is buried here is because her aunt is here. She liked the look of the place. I think she specified it in her will."

DeLucia walked out across the well-kept field. He walked toward a section of high walls filled with crypts.

"We've got Elizabeth Taylor's father here and Dean Martin's parents and Oscar Levant and a lot of Hollywood people," he said with pride. He pointed toward a wall in a shady spot filled with crypts:

Marilyn Monroe 1926–1962

There was a vase on the right. The red roses were bright and fresh. There was a small nick in the base of the crypt.

DeLucia had to get back to his office. Clarence Pierce, one of the owners of the mortuary, was out back and would be coming around soon. He would know more about the funeral.

"You might be interested in this," DeLucia said. "Joe DiMaggio shows up here once or twice a year. He comes unannounced. He pulls in, walks up to the crypt, stays a few minutes, and leaves. I've seen him a few times. We don't bother him. We respect people's privacy here."

Clarence Pierce appeared, a man in his seventies, tall, with a thin face. He had a soft voice and wore an appropriately dark suit.

"Oh, yes, that was some funeral," he said. "I got the first call from Mrs. Melson—you know, Miss Monroe's mother's caretaker. Then Mr. DiMaggio came over here later that night to see me. He made all the arrangements. We had just opened up that new chapel over there. I think that was the first funeral we ever held in that room. We received the body late one night, and Mr. DiMaggio stayed with it for a long time. Then I think he was here all the next day too. Then we had the services.

"Well, I'll tell you, there's never been anything like that here since. There were all those people around and the reporters outside the gates spilling over on the streets and the helicopters flying all around on the outside. Walter Winchell was in charge of all those reporters. He kept running around, telling them where to stand, telling the photographers how they could shoot pictures, telling all the reporters who everybody was. I listened to him myself because I didn't know who all those people were. I had only seen Mr. DiMaggio before the services.

"I can't tell you how long the services took. But it really wasn't very long. Then they all cleared out except for Mr. DiMaggio. He didn't leave for a long time. Then he left, finally, and that was all there was to it."

Norman Rosten, of all the people around Marilyn Monroe, seemed to have the purest and gentlest relationship with her. A bushy-haired novelist, playwright, and poet, he knew her not as an actress, celebrity, or lover but simply as a friend.

"She was mostly high-spirited. Her phone calls were lots of fun and she would be talking of what we would do when we saw each other next and she would always say, 'We have to live a little.' She was pensive at times. She did attempt suicide several times that I knew of. She tried it with heavy doses of sleeping pills.

"There seemed not to be anybody in her life at the time, between Joe DiMaggio and Arthur Miller. There was one man that we knew of, Henry Rosenfeld, a very decent guy, a businessman, who was quite taken with her at the time. He wanted to marry her but she wasn't interested.

"I only met Joe DiMaggio once. We were in a Hollywood restaurant—myself, my wife, Hedda, and Bill Inge and Marilyn. Marilyn saw Joe across the room and she waved. He came over. He seemed like a very likable kind of man, very straight, not complicated. She introduced us as friends from Brooklyn and she introduced Inge as a writer.

"I thought Joe and Marilyn had a good rapport. We didn't ask what happened between them. We didn't want to intrude. When she had the crackup and entered Payne-Whitney, he helped her. She turned to him. He was a tough cookie and she could depend on him. He could get things done and he did.

"Miller and DiMaggio were a lot alike. They were both stern. I don't want to say father figures. They were authority figures, also powerful men in terms of the public eye. DiMaggio was the king of baseball; Miller was a famous playwright. She gravitated toward power. This type of figure gives you security and absolution. With DiMaggio, she moved into a great circle of popular acceptance, into sports; with Miller, into the intellectual, literary world.

"I remember the last time we talked to Marilyn. It was the day before she died. She called here; it was a long call, sort of rambling. She seemed high. I spoke to her; my wife spoke to her. She talked about finishing her house, and how the flower beds were in, and about the new furniture that was coming. Still, it was like a person talking to you with a subliminal message. Underneath what she meant was something else. She said, 'I'm going to see you soon. We'll go to the theater. We'll go down and see a play in Washington.' That's what probably started a lot of the rumors about the Kennedys. She was going to Washington in 1962 to see a play, not them. An old friend, Henry Rosenfeld, was to escort her.

"That famous final telephone call—her hand found on the receiver. My feeling is she was calling her analyst; that's who you call when you are in trouble. Everyone wrote that she might have been calling the Kennedys, this brother or that one. DiMaggio? Why not? It wouldn't have been out of character. Marilyn didn't often talk of Joe with us but she did mention her honeymoon and the trip to Korea. She started out by saying how cold it was. Then she suddenly said, 'I cried on my honeymoon.' I asked her what she meant. She didn't answer. That was the end of it.

"I really didn't know Joe. I met him only that once, as I say, but I thought some of the things said about Joe and Marilyn were unfair. The press tried to make him out as some kind of clod. That wasn't fair. Joe had none of the subtlety of show business people. He was a decent sort of guy. She always felt that way about him. She respected him and leaned on him. Something had evidently gone wrong with the marriage, but a loyalty remained between them."

Sid Luckman, the former star quarterback of the Chicago Bears, is a close friend of DiMaggio's.

"Joe and I are like brothers. I love the man. I think I am as close to him as anyone on this earth. When he broke up with Marilyn in 1954 I was the first one he called. He came to Miami Beach and he spent ten days with me at the Fountainebleau. He had tremendous affection for her. It took him a long time to get over it.

"Then in 1962, when she died, he didn't come out of his house for six weeks. I was on the coast with the Bears. I called him. I convinced him he had to start living again. He had to get out. He finally agreed. He loved her desperately and he was devastated."

Some few months ago, more than twelve years after Marilyn's death, Luckman kidded Joe about remarrying. He reminded him that he wasn't getting any younger, that he needed a good woman to take care of him.

"I'll never remarry again," said DiMaggio.

"It wasn't with any pain that he said that," Luckman recalled. "It was simply a fact. The man had been hurt twice in marriage. He probably loved his first wife and he loved Marilyn. But he had two unhappy marriages. He wouldn't chance it again."

20: The Greatest

Bob Fishel, vice-president of the Yankees, has been with the team since 1954. One of his many jobs is to organize the annual Old Timers' Day festivities. It is often a difficult task, complicated by drunken old players, freeloading friends, bruised egos, and padded expense accounts. Fun for the fans, it's rarely that for the man who puts it together.

"Joe's never been any trouble at these things. He does whatever we ask of him. He never hits us for extra expenses or asks us to pick up special tabs. He is always a perfect gentleman. There is just one consideration and it was always honored—until 1968. Joe is proud of his record, his importance, and his hold on Yankee fans. When we introduced all the old great players, we always introduced Joe last.

"Mickey Mantle was retiring, so this was his last Old Timers' Day. Michael Burke was president of the Yankees then. I don't know if it was his idea or not. I know I went along with it. I'm sorry now I did. Mantle even came to me before the game and said, 'Don't do it, Bob.' We did it anyway. We introduced all the players and then we introduced DiMaggio. We had saved Mantle for last because he was retiring. We thought it would be a nice gesture. The applause for Joe was tremendous, as always. Then we introduced Mantle. The applause was greater and it went on and on and on. Somebody timed it at about ten minutes. It was incredible.

"DiMaggio just stood off to the side. You could see he was embarrassed. We didn't try to hurt him. It was more kids than grownups in the stands and they simply knew Mantle and maybe didn't remember DiMaggio. Mickey was quitting and we wanted to give him the last hurrah. It hurt Joe a lot. Our relationship has never been the same."

Joe DiMaggio played only thirteen full seasons because of the war, so the statistics do not reveal his greatness. Certainly his record was impressive—batting average .325, with a high of .381 and a low of .263; 131 triples; 389 doubles; 361 home runs; 4,529 putouts. He led the league

205

twice in runs batted in and twice in home runs, and he was voted the most valuable player three times. Ten of those thirteen seasons he led the Yankees to pennant wins—and on to championships all but one of those times.

Yet neither his leadership nor his excellence would be obvious from the record books, even from the amazingly low total of 105 physical errors he was charged with (as few as one during a whole season) and the 1,390 runs he scored (traveling around the bases for more than a thousand miles). The real greatness of Joe D had to be witnessed to be appreciated. Few who played with him or saw him could ever forget.

Eddie Yost was a ballplayer for almost two decades, mainly for the Washington Senators. A friendly man, stocky and bald now, he is wise in the ways of the game. He sat in the dugout at Al Lang Field in St. Petersburg in his coach's uniform and talked of his days of defensing third base against Joe DiMaggio.

"He was the best all-around player there was in my time; there's no doubt about that. When he went from first to third it was a picture. When he hit a triple he would make it a triple in the first fifteen feet, not the last. I mean he would get out of the box so fast and be running so hard in the first fifteen feet that it gave him the big edge. He ran a lot of doubles into triples in those first fifteen.

"Once in a while he would hit a triple or get to third base on a play and I would say 'Hi' to him and he would say 'Hi' back but that was it. With some other guys you could stand there and have a long conversation about their families or the weather or the crowd or the peanut vendor or anything. Not with DiMaggio. That's probably why he was so good. He wouldn't listen to chatter. His mind was where it should be, on the game, not on having a good conversation on the ball field.

"I've been to a few of those old timers' games and I've been around spring training a little bit with him, and we kid around about the old days and the old pitchers. But you just don't treat him the same as you treat another old ball-player. Hell, he's Joe DiMaggio. He's the best there was and you treat him with a lot of respect."

DiMaggio had become even more reclusive after Marilyn's death in 1962. But in the spring of 1968 he suddenly gave up his seclusion. He surfaced as a vice-president of the Oakland A's, and he became more visible and available. He dined in public more, appeared at more banquets.

The following year baseball decided to honor its past heroes with a testimonial dinner in Washington, D.C. It was the one hundredth anniversary of the game. A national contest had been held to select the greatest players and the dinner would be capped by the announcement of the results of the four categories—greatest players ever, greatest living players; then the single Greatest Player Ever and the Greatest Living Player. Among the guests were Secretary of State William Rogers, Associate Justice Byron White of the Supreme Court, astronaut Frank Borman, and assorted congressmen, senators, and other dignitaries.

Baseball Commissioner Bowie Kuhn, a large, imposing figure in his black tie and dinner jacket, introduced astronaut Borman as the person who would present the major awards. When only two awards remained, the room quieted. One award would go to Babe Ruth. The other would be for the greatest living player.

"The award for the greatest living player," said Borman, "goes to Joe DiMaggio."

"When it was all over we gathered in a large room," Hank Greenberg remembered. "There must have been a dozen television cameras around. We were all being interviewed. The room was filled with radio men and press. I don't think I ever saw more press in one place in my life. We all got a little attention. Joe got most of it. This was his night. No one else made both of those teams—greatest ever, greatest living—and then to be named the Greatest Living Player. It had to be his night. When you're playing, awards don't seem like much. Then you get older and all of it becomes more precious, more important, more significant. It is nice to be remembered. When you're sixty or so, maybe that's all you've got."

The centennial dinner had been a smashing success, so Commissioner Kuhn decided to honor the award winners with a dinner in Los Angeles the following January. Arthur Richman, promotions director of the Mets and one of DiMaggio's closest pals, recalled the ceremony.

"Joe asked me if I was going. I told him I would be there and I'd pick him up when he flew in from San Francisco. The dinner was at the Beverly Hilton and I arranged for Joe to have his suite there. The whole thing was going to be on television and the commissioner hoped it would be an annual affair for baseball, if it went well.

"The dinner was long and dreary and it bombed. It was about midnight or so when we went into the lounge for a couple of drinks. Gene Mauch and Don Drysdale were sitting at the bar near us. They greeted Joe and that was about it. Joe and I just sat there, had a few drinks quietly, and talked about the dinner. About two in the morning Joe turned to me and said, 'Let's go get something to eat.' He paid the bill and we walked out.

"We jumped into a cab and told the guy to take us to a decent place. He said he knew just the perfect spot, a nice, little all-night restaurant; they made great ham and eggs there and it was out of the way. We rode a while and talked, and finally the cab stopped. Joe got out and looked across the street. Then he just stood there without moving. I had

208

no idea what it was all about. Then I looked across the street and noticed a cemetery. I looked at Joe and saw tears come to his eyes. 'What's the matter, Joe?' He looked over at me. 'Don't you know? This is where I got Marilyn.' "

During DiMaggio's career, rivals were constantly proclaimed new DiMaggios. In 1946 it was a power hitter from the Pittsburgh Pirates named Ralph Kiner. Like many others, he was immediately hailed as another Joe DiMaggio. Kiner couldn't field as well, however, nor did he have much skill at running or throwing. But he was a marvelous hitter with incredible strength. For close to a decade he was the heart of the Pittsburgh franchise. People would come to the games of the lowly Pirates merely to see him bat and would leave right after his last time at bat.

"I patterned myself after DiMaggio. I had the same kind of stance. I was a right-handed hitter and I held the bat high in the air, like he did. Joe had no stride at all into the ball; he would hold back and just crush it. That's the way I hit—short stride or no stride at all, trying to stay perfectly balanced so I could get everything into my swing.

"I got a good offer from the Yankees after I got out of school and I was about to take it. Then the Pirates came along and offered me more money and I signed with them. This was before the war and DiMaggio was still playing. I really forget now. Maybe I figured I would be better off if I didn't sign with the same team that DiMaggio was with. I knew there was only one DiMaggio.

"A couple of years ago I was with him at an old timers' thing in Chicago. We were all in the clubhouse getting dressed and Joe was over in the corner putting on his Yankee uniform, number five, and all of a sudden everyone seemed to stop and stare at him. I don't know why. It was just one of those things, the greatest player in the game, and even the other old ballplayers wanted to look at him

209

and wanted to see how he was doing after a lot of years out of baseball. Well, everybody was looking at him and he pulled on his pants leg and then he pulled on the other pants leg and he started pulling up his pants. The clubhouse man, Yosh Kowano, who has been there forever, saw us all standing there for that second watching DiMaggio and he yelled at the top of his voice, 'Okay, you guys, you can all stop looking at DiMaggio. He gets dressed the same as everybody else.' "

21: Joe's Town

Robert Spero is a vice-president of the Ogilvy and Mather advertising agency in Manhattan.

"One day the name of Joe DiMaggio just popped into my head. I had seen him play when I was a kid in Cleveland. It was just a name that stayed with me. It seemed to represent what we wanted.

"We had gotten the Bowery Savings Bank account and they asked us to develop a large campaign for them. They wanted a spokesman for the bank. They didn't want someone identified as an actor. They wanted a fresh face, someone with a clean, wholesome image, someone natural who could represent a large cross-section of New York. Somebody said something about the campaign reminding us of what New York used to be, the New York that was looked on as the finest city in the country, where all the kids in the Midwest and down South aimed for.

"I threw Joe's name out to the people at the Bowery and at the agency, and it was an instant smash.

"We got in touch with his New York lawyer, Julian

Rosenthal. He said Joe would be in town and we could meet for breakfast and talk over the deal.

"He walked into the place and he seemed so incredibly tall. He was so handsome and well built. I knew he would be a terrific success if we could get him. I was like a little kid. I was sweating a lot when we had that first conversation.

"Joe liked the idea and we told him we would work up a complete proposal. We met again and went over the storyboards with him. We told him what the job would involve. He reminded us he would never do or say anything that would damage his image. He wouldn't do a beer commercial or a cigarette commercial or be seen in an ad with a cigarette.

"After a while he seemed to like the whole idea of the campaign. We told him he would be working a lot with kids. He seemed to like that too. He went away and left the business dealings in the hands of his lawyer. We worked things out and Joe signed a contract. Everybody has been very happy with the results—the bank, Joe, us, and the public. About the only problem we have is finding him when we have a campaign to work up. Joe is a hard man to locate. We always start with his home in San Francisco, but he could be just about anywhere at any time. We usually have to find him first before we can set up a shooting schedule.

"I remember going home one night after the deal was made. I have a nine-year-old son named Josh. I told him we had just signed a famous ballplayer for a campaign. He guessed Joe DiMaggio. I was very impressed with the idea that a kid that age would still have such a strong identification with DiMaggio's name.

"All the kids in the ads are professional actors but they work very well with Joe. He is very warm with kids. He has a toughness and a coldness around strangers, and he sort

211

of guards himself, but all that seems to break down with the kids. They all adore him.

"I remember the first ads we filmed. It was in Yankee Stadium and you could feel the tension all around as Joe began working. He was very stiff and the ads weren't very good. He had to loosen up a little, get used to the whole thing and just be the Joe DiMaggio we all remembered. In the beginning there were some tough sessions. This kind of thing can be very hard work for a guy who isn't skilled in the business. You can't just walk in, say a couple of words, and be gone in fifteen minutes. It doesn't work that way— it's a full day's work. Joe gave us a full day of work all the time.

"After a while he began loosening up, working better, and feeling more comfortable with everything he did. In the beginning he just did what the director wanted and that was the end of it. Then he started getting familiar with the whole operation. He began making suggestions and getting more interested in all the aspects. One day he asked if he could see the film before it was approved. We started to run things back on tape so he could see what he was doing as he did it. He liked that. He asked for more takes so he could do things better and wouldn't let it go until he was satisfied he had done as well as he could.

"We filmed one segment in Fort Lauderdale, at the Yankee ball park down there, and he was working with guys he knew—Gil McDougald, Tommy Henrich, and Elston Howard. That was a very good one. He was loose, they were loose, and a lot of warmth and personality came through. Joe has now gotten to the point where almost all the segments he does are excellent.

"As time went on, he became more and more concerned with the excellence of his work. It got to be sort of a challenge to him. He felt he was a professional now. He got

212

very involved. It was just like when he was playing ball. Joe DiMaggio has a lot of character. He wouldn't just take the money and run."

When DiMaggio comes to New York he is invariably met by a friend of forty years' standing, Ernie Sisto.

"I pick Joe up at the airport a lot when he comes in to shoot those Bowery Bank commercials. He did all right with that, the son of a gun, considering he never liked talking on television."

A retired *New York Times* photographer, Sisto met DiMaggio when he was the Yankees' hot rookie.

"We got real friendly right away. He was a raw kid, very shy, a lot like me, and we just got along good. I can't explain it, but he just took a liking to a jerk like me.

"I hated to annoy him for pictures but he understood. He knew he was a symbol, especially for the kids, and he would pose, but he liked to pose in the dugout, away from the fans, instead of on the field. He was embarrassed to stand out there on the field and pose for pictures. Joe never wanted any publicity. One time he went to a hospital to visit a kid that was dying. I remember his name, Joe Klein, and his father said the kid idolized Joe. He called me to come along so he could give the kid some pictures. He made me promise one thing. 'Don't hand these pictures to the *Times*.' I never did. Joe just wasn't one for publicity.

"If he's a friend of yours he is a very loyal guy. There isn't anything he wouldn't do. You know why we got along, why Joe likes me after all these years? I never cashed in on anything I ever did with Joe DiMaggio."

In New York DiMaggio usually stays at the Americana and often goes across the street to the Stage Delicatessen for a sandwich. If a truck driver jumps out of his cab and presses him for an autograph—as has happened—Joe will stand there, in the middle of the avenue, and sign the torn piece of paper excitedly being offered.

In the evenings he will dine with friends at their homes or else he will have an Italian dinner at a restaurant near the hotel called La Scala. In the far corner of the place, close to the little bar and the kitchen, is a small table—his. Above it on the wall is a gallery of DiMaggio pictures, cartoons, drawings, box scores, trophies. There is even a cabinet of baseballs, each autographed by DiMaggio and inscribed with the date and significance of the event commemorated.

When DiMaggio comes in, the first thing he does is go back into the kitchen. He kids with the staff and the owner, Arturo. He looks in the pots and decides what he'd like that day.

On the street, heads turn everywhere. "It's Joe's Town," Toots Shor once said. And it is still true.

22: The Man They Save for Last

For all his baseball accomplishments and fame, the one thing that always eluded DiMaggio was a substantial role in the sport after he retired as a player. There never seemed to be a real baseball job for the Yankee Clipper.

Commissioner Bowie Kuhn had stung Joe with a half-hearted offer of an undefined job in 1970. Three years later the Yankee management, headed by Michael Burke, hinted at wanting DiMaggio back in the organization. Then they changed their minds. "The incumbents identified more strongly with Mantle," Burke said later. Club politics were the problem; they prevented the offer to DiMaggio and later kept Burke from buying the Yankees from CBS, with Joe as one of his partners. There was also the matter of that Old Timers' Day in 1968, when the Yankees had publicly embarrassed DiMaggio.

Thus in 1974, when the Yankees invited DiMaggio to attend the old timers' festivities honoring Mantle and Whitey Ford for their election to the Hall of Fame, they were a little nervous.

"Joe is a very loyal guy," says Joe Reichler, assistant to the commissioner of baseball. "If he is your friend he will go out of his way for you—and he expects you to go out of your way for him. But there is one trait about him that I always found tough to take. Joe harbors a grudge. He'll cut you off dead, and that will be the end of it. He's done that to a lot of guys through the years. He doesn't care how close he may have been with you at one time—if he thinks you did him dirty, that's it. Look at that feud with Toots. No two guys were closer. Bingo, Toots said something he didn't like and that was the end."

Shor had passed a remark about Marilyn Monroe. DiMaggio never said anything about it. He simply never said anything to Shor for years afterward. The Yankee front office had cause to worry about its strained relationship with the great star.

DiMaggio—dealing, as he often did, through intermediaries—sent word that he would be there for the ceremonies. He arrived in the crowded clubhouse early the next afternoon. He seemed more distracted and taut than usual. Pitcher Ralph Terry came over to him and asked for an autograph for a youngster injured in an auto accident. DiMaggio signed his name carefully. Baseballs were passed to him and he autographed them all. Then some old teammates drifted over—Charlie Keller, Tommy Henrich, Yogi Berra, Billy Martin, Allie Reynolds, Vic Raschi, Whitey

215

Ford. Joe Page was there too, looking thin and quite ill. The banter was warm. The young reporters and broadcasters approached with trepidation, asking softly for interviews. DiMaggio responded easily and talked graciously of the skills of Mantle and Ford.

Then he took off his shirt and asked the old clubhouse man, Pete Sheehy, for a baseball undershirt. He pulled off a ring, handed it to a friend, and then went about dressing.

Most of the old timers were in the dugout when DiMaggio emerged. He looked for an empty seat and sat down next to Allie Reynolds. He talked with Reynolds, staring straight ahead at the field. Suddenly he grew silent.

Mantle and Ford were introduced first to huge cheers from a loving crowd of fifty thousand people. Then came the others, the Yankees of summers past—the gray-haired, heavy, and jowly men who had performed with such excellence for so many years: Bauer, Woodling, McDougald, Martin, Raschi, Lopat, Reynolds, Collins, Brown.

Casey Stengel was introduced, three days past his eighty-fourth birthday. He danced nimbly up the steps of the dugout, waved his fingers behind his back, and literally skipped to his place in the receiving line.

"And now," said Yankee broadcaster Frank Messer, "the man we always save for last . . ." The roar began somewhere around first base, rolled through the right-field stands, and spread through the park. Everyone was standing. DiMaggio jogged to the long line of players, waving his cap in acknowledgment of the ovation.

He kissed Mrs. Gehrig and Mrs. Ruth and shook hands with all the others in the long line of baseball celebrities—Commissioner Bowie Kuhn, retired American League president Joe Cronin, Stengel, Ford, Mickey Mantle, Willie Mays.

Then came the ritual of the game. The old players would

216

walk to home plate and swing a bat against a ball, and the crowd would lose itself in reverie.

It was DiMaggio's turn. The ball floated up to the plate and he cracked it hard. The sound of it shocked almost everyone. The umpire pointed to foul territory and DiMaggio resumed his stance in the batter's box. Mel Allen sat on a small chair next to the dugout, holding his microphone. DiMaggio hit the next pitch. "There's a high drive out toward left field; it's going, it's going . . ." The ball bounced in the dirt track ringing the outfield and landed against the concrete wall. DiMaggio, head down, smoothly jogged to first base.

Standing at first, he was serious and intent. He was in a baseball game now, an old timers' game, a meaningless contest to be sure, but the pride was obvious in his carriage —the determination of the man, the compulsive drive to excel, to triumph. Joe DiMaggio was home.

23: A Talk with DiMaggio

"We can talk," Joe said when I saw him at the baseball writers' dinner in New York in January 1974, "but I can't help you very much."

I asked him for his phone number and said I would call him in the spring. In March he was in Florida for a golf tournament at the Doral Country Club, and I was at spring training with the Yankees. We made a date.

I sat on the front lawn at the Doral. There were Arnold Palmer, Lee Trevino, Jack Nicklaus in orange slacks and a yellow shirt. Where was Joe DiMaggio?

He appeared suddenly out of the crowd—still tall and

handsome, his thick wavy hair white, his body lean and hard as he approached sixty. He had on a red sports shirt, open at the throat, and gray slacks, and he wore golf shoes. We sat down in the shade of the clubhouse and talked.

Earlier I had spoken to Whitey Ford, who had just finished playing a tournament with DiMaggio. Ford told me Joe had said his handicap was eighteen; he didn't believe it and asked me to check it out.

"Yeah, that's about it," said DiMaggio. "It's a funny thing about golf. I never played the game at all when I was playing baseball; I thought it would hurt my swing. Then I quit and my friend Lefty O'Doul got me interested. Now I play almost every day, as much as I can. I make a lot of these tournaments. I enjoy the game but I don't enjoy the travel to get there. That's why I quit baseball. I didn't want to travel any more. Now look at me. I'm traveling just as much." He laughed.

"I enjoy golf," he said. "I really do. It's a lot of fun and I enjoy playing with the people I play with."

As much as baseball?

He looked out over the golf course for a moment, smiled weakly at his friend Bob Barrasso, and thought for a moment.

"This is fun," he said, "but baseball was my life." He paused again. "I was six years old when I started playing baseball. It was all I knew. It was all I ever wanted to know. I was good at it and I learned to handle the game. I handled the aches and pains and I handled the pressures. I was always a conservative-type fellow. I shied away from things having to do with the limelight. I just enjoyed playing the game."

There was a brief sadness in DiMaggio's eyes. It was as if, at sixty, he wished he could go back there again—be twenty-five for a day, swing hard at Bobby Feller, drive a baseball high into the seats, glide back for a catch, stretch a single into a double, feel the grass under his feet, the sweat, the noise in that cavernous stadium.

"I remember when I did that first television commercial some years back for Brylcreem. I didn't know what I was doing out there. It's a little better now with the Bowery commercials and the Mr. Coffee ads. I am a little more used to it. But it's not like playing ball. I'm still a little uncertain when I do the commercials. On the ball field I was never uncertain. I knew what I was doing out there."

Casey Stengel?

Joe's face twisted in a strange smile. "The old man had his ways and I had mine. I don't want to say any more about that."

What was his relationship like with the Yankees in recent years?

"It was different when Topping and Webb were there. I knew them well. These are all new people.

"Managing wasn't for me," he continued. "I didn't want to handle players. I didn't want to travel with a ball club, to put up with the hours, with night ball. I don't know, running the game might have been fun. That might have been a challenge. I might have enjoyed that."

DiMaggio seemed to want to say that he would have liked to have been asked. He probably would not have accepted. He probably would not have given up the golf courses, the freedom, the unstructured life, for the grind of a manager's job. Still, it would have been nice to have been asked, if only to turn it down.

"I guess I'm sour on baseball now," DiMaggio said. "I guess I'm not going to do anything any more to help them. I've been embarrassed too many times now. They told me they wanted me to work in a public-relations job. They said I could represent baseball at special events. They said I would be free to make my own schedule. It was all left hanging. Then they said they would pay me fifteen thousand dollars. That was insulting. I just felt that they had taken advantage of me; they had used me. They told everybody they were trying to hire me and when it came time to make an offer, they made a pitiful offer. It was unpleasant. I don't think I would care to work for a man like Bowie Kuhn anyway."

DiMaggio always had one secret baseball ambition.

"I always thought about an ownership situation. I always thought that might be something I would enjoy. It wouldn't demand all my time and it would allow me to stay with the game."

In January 1973 Michael Burke, the president of the Yankees, had been putting together a syndicate to purchase control of the club from the Columbia Broadcasting System. His major partner in the venture was to be Cleveland shipping industrialist George Steinbrenner III.

"It was at the baseball dinner in New York," DiMaggio said. "Burke approached me and said he would like to talk to me in the Yankees' suite. It had been hinted to me by friends that an ownership situation was possible."

Burke was collecting partners as rapidly as he could. He thought DiMaggio's name and money would make the task easier.

"They told me to meet them in the suite and I did. Steinbrenner was there. I hadn't met him before and didn't know him. They explained the deal. They said they were getting a large group together. They wanted to know if I was interested. I asked them what my position would be. I wanted to know what they expected of me, outside of the investment. We talked for about fifteen minutes. I told them I was interested and would talk to my lawyer, Edward Bennett Williams, and see what he had to say about it. Burke said they would get back to me in a short time. They would keep me informed of the progress of the deal. They never did. I read about the final sale in the papers. That burned me up."

DiMaggio's voice—controlled, careful—has a way of rising when he is angry. His voice became thinner.

"That was my last chance at getting back into baseball. That was the end of it. That kind of thing will never happen to me again."

DiMaggio leaned back in his chair. He looked at his watch, stood up, and reached into his golf bag. He pulled out his putter, sank a few imaginary putts, and said, "I'd better be getting out to that practice green."

He paused for a moment.

"I had a wonderful career. I have very pleasant memories of it. People have been very kind to me since. I enjoy my retirement. I play a lot of golf; I have a lot of friends. I have no regrets. Some things happened to me, some people disappointed me, but you get over that. I still enjoy the game. I still enjoy watching some of the kids I might have helped a little. When I was in Oakland for that time I worked with kids like Sal Bando and Rick Monday and Reggie Jackson. Jackson couldn't catch a fly ball. Look at him now. He's about the best there is."

"Okay, Joe," his partner said, "let's get on over there.

DiMaggio began walking toward the golf carts. He held the putter in his right hand and put a yellow hat on his head with his left. As he walked out from the clubhouse heads began turning.

"Hey, Joe. Hi, Joe. Joe D, Joe D," people shouted.

He waved and smiled at them. Several people rushed over.

"I was there that night in Cleveland, Joe," one pudgy, bald-headed man half-shouted. "I was there. You hit those bullets and Keltner robbed you and I was there."

"Were you?" DiMaggio said.

"Yeah, I was just a kid then, thirteen, fourteen maybe, and I was rooting for you to get a hit because it would have been fun to see you go all season with a hit every game. I remember it, Joe, I really do."

"I do too," said DiMaggio, softly.